FINAL RESOLUTION

The Separation of Truth and Lies in the Bible

Cohane Michael Levi

Published By Levitical Communications Inc.
P.O Box 1324 Bear. DE. 19701

ISBN: 0-97011344-7

Library of Congress Control Number:

2003110456

Printed in the United States by Morris Publishing
3212 East Highway 30
Kearney, NE 68847
1-800-650-7888

TABLE OF CONTENTS

ABOUT THE AUTHOR

Cohane Michael Levi was born to Shmaryah Levi (Eddie Young Sr.) and Miryom Levi (Mae Young) in New York City and was raised in Brownsville, Brooklyn. He has nine siblings and is a devoted husband and a proud, dedicated father. He attended Boys High School located in the Bedford Stuyvesant section of Brooklyn. He later attended Morgan State College in Baltimore, Maryland for two years. He received his Bachelor of Arts degree from City College in New York and his Masters of Science degree in Special Education from the Graduate School of Education at City College.

Cohane Michael, as he is known, has served the Israelite community in his capacity as a teaching Priest/Minister for over twenty five years. He is well known as a scholar of Israelite history, as well as the hebrew language and heritage. He has worked as a principal of the Israelite Institute in New York City and in Guyana, South America and has taught secondary school in the Guyana Ministry of Education. He also has taught in the New York City Board of Education Public school system

In 1978 he migrated to Guyana where he has established an Israelite community and erected the first Hebrew Israelite Cultural Center in the region. For over fifteen years he has provided information about Israelite history and culture through radio and television broadcasts in the Caribbean and South America. He has also given lectures in many colleges and universities.

Cohane Michael is the founder of Levitical Communications Inc., which is dedicated to the spread of Israelite history and culture among Africans in the Diaspora. He has traveled extensively throughout North America, the Caribbean and to Israel in Northeast Africa. He is well known throughout the Israelite community worldwide and is highly respected.

ACKNOWLEDGEMENTS

Many Prayers have been offered to the Creator of Heaven and Earth for the manifestation of this book. Therefore, it is incumbent upon me to thank The Holy One of Israel, first and foremost, for the publication of the manuscript which has made this book a reality.

Yahwah truly helps those who help themselves. However, quite often his help comes to us through other people. Without the assistance of Nasik Immanuel Ben Yehudah and the staff of Communicators Press, this book would not be in existence. I would like to express my profound appreciation and gratitude to Ahtur Yatsiliel. I would also like to thank Sister Simah Babb, Claire Lugo (Oliyah) and Tamekyah Levi for their relentless typing and editorial work which resulted in the completion of this book. Last, but not least, I thank Malcha Levi, my children and family for their continuous encouragement and support.

May this divinely inspired work serve as an instrument to enlighten and restore Israelites and mankind to their Creator. Thus, may the dissemination of the Truth contained in the pages of this book bring justice to all those who struggle for Truth and Righteousness sake. Let it also bring vindication to our ancestors who lived and died for its noble cause.

AUTHOR'S NOTES

The word "God" is used loosely nowadays to represent any God. As such; this word and the very concept does not exist in the Hebrew language or in the original Holy Scriptures. Whenever the word "God is spelled with an upper case letter (G) it will denote a reference to the Creator only. The use of a lower case letter (g) will always denote a false God.

The Creator of Heaven and Earth told the Levites to put his name upon his chosen people Israel in Numbers 6:24, "The Priestly Blessing" which says, "May Yahwah Bless Thee and Keep Thee. May Yahwah Cause His Face to Shine Upon Thee and Be Gracious Unto Thee. May Yahwah Lift Up His Countenance Upon Thee and Give Thee Peace."

Yet, the True name of the Creator, *Yahwah* which reflects His Eternal Oneness has been deliberately removed from usage in the Bible. Thus, replaced by the term "God" - a more modern and generally accepted term among most religions. More often than not, in assuming "God" is whatever or whomsoever is intended, with no direct understanding of or connection to the Ancient Biblical heritage.

INTRODUCTION

Come let us reason together. Let us reason together about one of the most sensitive topics in the whole world, The Bible. Within the context of the bible is the most sensitive topic or subject in the entire universe. Who is God?

Even though the Bible is a history book, millions of people view the Bible in a religious manner. So many people refuse to discuss the subject of God, which is often viewed to them as their religion.

It is a difficult subject to discuss because the word God means different things or beings to different people. For many people, the Bible, God, Jesus.. are all topics that are highly sensitive, because they are rooted more in emotions, than any historical/biblical fact. Many people have simply inherited their beliefs as a part of their familial/cultural legacy. "I believe because 'mama'/daddy/grandmama or granddaddy was a..' and then simply, fill in the blank. The majority of the people who read the Bible, and/or profess to believe it, often know little about it, or its historical truths. In fact, very few people know of their own religious teachings and history.

Yet in order to fully understand the Bible and the particular topics in this work, I implore you the reader, to divorce your emotions from the subsequent discussion. Allow yourself for a time to read and consider the information that will be presented, along with the supporting scriptures, simply on the basis of "is it fact?"

Again, when it comes to the Bible a great number of people who read it are extremely limited in their ability to discern the material in-depth. Some have only read the Old Testament in length and some have greater knowledge of the New Testament and little or no thorough understanding of the Old Testament.

As a result, the Bible has become the most read yet least intellectually explored book in the world - at least across religious and ethnic lines.

Therefore I personally commend all who are courageous enough to read this text and enter into a reasoning of the minds. It is vitally important to hear the entire matter presented here. It is all the evidence, which is factual that establishes the truth. To only hear part of one's viewpoint and draw a judgment or conclusion is dishonesty.

Therefore, my humble request is that we engage in our reasoning with a willingness to challenge our intellect as we discuss the Bible. This book will focus on the Bible as a complete document and discuss the relationship between the Old Testament and New Testament. It will examine the significance of any similarities or differences. It will also analyze the process, which developed into the Bible canonization. The research contained in this work will also focus on the historical, cultural and linguistic perspective, within the Bible. We shall also scrutinize these dimensions in respect to the impact, which the Bible has made upon the minds of the world.

THE NAME

The Hebrew concept of GOD differs from the Greek concept. The translations of ideas from any language to another can never be expressed or conveyed identically in another language. Therefore, two entirely different languages such as Hebrew and Greek, can never have the exact spiritual concept, because they did not derive from the same spiritual source. There is and can be no spiritual connection.

> *And God spoke unto Moses, and said unto him, I am the Lord:*
>
> *And I appeared unto Abraham, unto Isaac, and unto Jacob, by the name of God Almighty, but by my name YAHWAH was I not known to them.*
>
> ***Exodus 6:2-3***

Although, many names, phrases and titles are used to identify and describe the CREATOR, there is only one personal name, of GOD. It is יהוה (YAHWAH). In the Holy Scriptures HE is called the CREATOR, the MOST HIGH, the HOLY ONE OF YISRAEL, ADONAI, LORD, ELOHIM, LORD OF HOSTS, KING OF ISRAEL, LORD OF LORDS, GOD OF Gods or ABBAH(father), to mention a few. However, YAHWAH is the only personal name used by the CREATOR Himself and given to His people Yisrael. The three following versions or pronounciation of the divine name have these distinctions.

יה YAH- A shortened version, has <u>one</u> syllable. It is an abbreviated form of Yahwah

יהוה YAHWAH- Pronounced YAH-WAH has <u>two</u> syllables

יהוה YAHOWAH- Pronounced YAH-HO-WAH has <u>three</u> syllables

These are the most commonly used pronounciations among Israelites. More importantly they are recognized as having derived from the same Hebrew root or word. The true name of the CREATOR is recorded hundreds of times throughout the Old Testament. And, yet translators of the Bible have failed to convey the correct name of GOD in the translations. There is indisputable evidence that shows a deliberate conspiracy to conceal the name of the GOD, His identity and to eradicate the existence of His chosen people Israel.

> *A Song or Psalm of Asaph. Keep not thou silence, O God: hold not thy peace, and be not still, O God.*
>
> *For, lo, thine enemies make a tumult: and they that hate thee have lifted up the head.*
>
> *They have taken crafty counsel against thy people, and consulted against thy hidden ones.*
>
> *They have said, Come, and let us cut them off from being a nation; that the name of Israel may be no more in remembrance.*
>
> *For they have consulted together with one consent: they are confederate against thee:*
>
> ***Psalms 83:1-5***

There are a number of gods whose names are associated with other religious books. The Quoran is associated with God whom Muslims call Allah. The Hindus have many gods associated with their Veda's or religious books. Idols and graven images represent their various dieties. In similar fashion, Christians produced the New Testament associated with Jesus. The European converts to Judaism adopted the Tanach (Torah) and Holy Scriptures associated with the Creator Yahwah.

In a historical sense the Hebrew Scriptures pre-date the Vedas, Quoran and New Testament. The GOD Yahwah of the Holy Scriptures has the distinction of being spirit and Eternal. On the contrary, the new gods associated with Vedas and New Testament are idols and in the Christian teachings, a dead man. On the other hand, Muslims regard Allah as the Creator. However, the Torah or Laws of Moses and the Holy Scriptures and prophets are acknowledged as forerunners to the Quoran.

The people of Israel were empowered with the knowledge of the name of their Creator, Yahwah long before any of these schools of thought existed.

It is important to understand, there is power in the true name, Yahwah. Any people disconnected from the name of their Creator is weakened. In order to subdue the Children of Israel, the name and knowledge of their Creator, Yahwah had to be removed and replaced. The name of any god points to a particular people and geography; when the Children of Israel become empowered with the name of their GOD they become aware of who they are and where they came from.

In a greater sense, the name Yahwah in the Bible is the foundation required to comprehend the concepts, principles and events recorded. The understanding and concepts associated with the name Yahwah provides the fundamentals necessary to analyze the Bible. When we know the true name Yahwah and read the Bible it is unlikely we will be led astray from the true Creator to a man-created god.

The question about what is the name of Creator is indisputable. The name has been carved in stone from ancient times and is proclaimed emphatically just too many times to deny. This blatant false claim has only existed because it has gone unchallenged for over a thousand years. The spread of Christianity has dominated religious thought. Christian propaganda has permeated music, theater, literature, education and influences every aspect of our existence.

What's in a name? A name is an identification. A name can also describe someone or something. In Exodus the Creator also declares that He is the "power" (Elohim) of Abraham, Isaac and Jacob. The Creator has a name which is unique. He is distinguished by attributes and powers which are beyond human comprehension. He is the Ruler and Possessor of the universe. He is the Eternal One. In Exodus 20:1 speaking before all Israel in mount Sinai, Yah proclaims, "I am Yahwah, thy power

(Eloheh'cha) who brought thee up out of the land of Egypt and out of the house of bondage."

Numerous false gods are recorded in the Old Testament. Yet Israel was commanded not to worship any of them. In fact, the Law of Moses specifically prohibited even mentioning the names of other gods.

> *When the LORD thy God shall cut off the nations from before thee, whither thou goest to possess them, and thou succeedest them, and dwellest in their land;*
>
> *Take heed to thyself that thou be not snared by following them, after that they be destroyed from before thee; and that thou inquire not after their gods, saying, How did these nations serve their gods? even so will I do likewise.*
>
> *Thou shalt not do so unto the LORD thy God: for every abomination to the LORD, which he hateth, have they done unto their gods; for even their sons and their daughters they have burnt in the fire to their gods.*
>
> ***Deuteronomy 12:29-31***

On these point alone we can see how important the knowledge of the true name of Yahwah is to those who worship Him. There is no acceptable substitue for those who Worship Yahwah in spirit and in truth.

The name of Yah in the Old Testament is not only proclaimed, but, is also connected to divine events wonderfully manifested. As a result of his power the Creator's name will become revered and renown above all names.

We live in a world where people have become more important than the Creator who made them, and their names receive more notariety, respect and praise. Names like Muhammed Ali, Michael Jordan, Tiger Woods, Ophrah Winfrey, Janet Jackson and Madonna, to name a few, are known throughout the world. People idolize celebrities and superstar entertainers whose names are advertised, promoted and worshipped. Yet, Yahwah who made them, us and everything in the universe is virtually unknown. Things are terribly wrong because the removal of the knowledge of God's true name has impacted on the entire world adversely. These precepts, Psalms 148:13-14 and Psalm 150:6, tell us that humanity must reverse the trend and abandon the practice of exalting the names of men above the name of Yahwah..

> *Let them praise the name of the Lord: for his name alone is excellent; his glory is above the earth and heaven.*
>
> *He also exalteth the horn of his people, the praise of all his saints; even of the children of Israel, a people near unto him. Halleluyah!*
>
> ***Psalms 148:13-14***
>
> *Let every thing that hath breath praise the Lord. Halleluyah!*
>
> ***Psalm 150:1-6***

It is interesting to note that "halleluyah" consists of two Hebrew words. "Hallel" which means praise and the abbreviated form of the Creator's name "Yahwah". The combination of those two words, results in the phrase "praise Yah." Whenever anyone mentions the phrase, "halleluyah" they are actually voicing praise to the Creator, in the original Hebrew, using the correct Hebrew name of the Creator.

Again, the Old Testament contains example after example of the correct name of Yahwah and the correct form in which it is to be used. Further examples also clearly differentiate between the personal name of the Creator, Yahwah, and some of the numerous attributes that can be used to describe Him (Exodus 6:2, as referenced earlier, provides an excellent example of the Creator proclaiming His personal name.)

The original name proclaimed and declared by the Creator in the Old Testament is challenged only in the New Testament. Nowhere in the

Old Testament or Holy Scriptures is the name of the Creator in dispute. In cases where a different title or attribute is used, each case always refers to the Creator and same source. The discrepancy or problem only arises when one attempts to associate the New Testament deity with the Old Testament personage. Upon further examination, we will see that there are two different personages described: one Divine; one man-made.

It is here that we deduce that an investigation is necessary surrounding the issue of what is the true name of the Creator. This is one way to establish where the Truth and Lie exist within the Bible. There are clearly two different gods and contradicting concepts about them found within documents of the Bible. The Bible, in its present, King James version, is the source of the confusion. The King James, with its continued attempt to reconcile the Old Testament and the New Testament fuels the controversy.

The personal name of the Creator and the proper undersanding of His name and identification of His attributes is a consistent concept in the precepts and throughout the Holy Scriptures. In order for this to be realized the personal name the Creator must be the same everywhere in the Bible.

> *Thus saith the Lord, thy redeemer, and he that formed thee from the womb, I am the Lord that maketh all things; that stretcheth forth the heavens alone; that spreadeth abroad the earth by myself;*
>
> *That frustrateth the tokens of the liars, and maketh diviners, mad; that turneth wise men backward, and maketh their knowledge foolish;*
>
> *That confirmeth the word of his servant, and performeth the counsel of his messengers; that saith to Jerusalem, Thou shalt be inhabited; and to the cities of Judah, Ye shall be built, and I will raise up the decayed places thereof:*
>
> ***Isaiah 44:24-26***

So, it becomes clear that the first order in discerning between the truth and the lies attributed to the Bible, is the correct understanding and use of the Creator, Yahwah's, name. With the various precepts that we have examined, we can see the consistency of the use of the Creator's name and as a result, just how far we have strayed from our correct understanding of Him.

Man alone is responsible for the name used in Christian writings to describe the Creator of the Universe. The CREATOR has never declared to anyone in any age that his name is Jesus or Yeshua. Yeshua is simply a discription of an attribute. The CREATOR as a supreme absolute Power is a DELIVERER, REDEEMER or SAVIOR. A Savior means someone capable of saving others. This attribute which is mentioned in several places in the Holy Scriptures is not used as a personal name for YAHWAH. The name YAHWAH is the only name ever given in Scripture as the personal of God. This name YAHWAH was declared by God ALMIGHTY Himself unto Moses.

Every deity on earth is associated with a particular people. In fact, in all cases, but one the deity was named by the people. The people also chose the god, created and even made the god. The concept of every false god on Earth has been created by a people some where and at sometime in the past. Along with the creation of a name for the deity a form of worship was developed.

On the other hand, the Creator revealed his name to Israel the people He chose for himself.

> *And Moses said unto God, Behold, when I come unto the children of Israel, and shall say unto them, The God of your fathers hath sent me unto you; and they shall say to me, What is his name? what shall I say unto them?*
>
> *And God said unto Moses, I AM THAT I AM: and he said, Thus shalt thou say unto the children of Israel, I AM hath sent me unto you.*

And God said moreover unto Moses, Thus shalt thou say unto the children of Israel, The LORD God of your fathers, the God of Abraham, the God of Isaac, and the God of Jacob, hath sent me unto you: this is my name for ever, and this is my memorial unto all generations.

Exodus 3:13-15

And thou shalt say unto Pharaoh, Thus saith the LORD, Israel is my son, even my firstborn:

And I say unto thee, Let my son go, that he may serve me: and if thou refuse to let him go, behold, I will slay thy son, even thy firstborn.

Exodus 4:22-23

But now thus saith the LORD that created thee, O Jacob, and he that formed thee, O Israel, Fear not: for I have redeemed thee, I have called thee by thy name; thou art mine.

When thou passest through the waters, I will be with thee; and through the rivers, they shall not overflow thee: when thou walkest through the fire, thou shalt not be burned; neither shall the flame kindle upon thee.

For I am the LORD thy God, the Holy One of Israel, thy Saviour: I gave Egypt for thy ransom, Ethiopia and Seba for thee.

Since thou was precious in my sight, thou hast been honourable, and I have loved thee: therefore will I give men for thee, and people for thy life.

Fear not: for I am with thee: I will bring thy seed from the east, and gather thee from the west;

I will say to the north, Give up; and to the south,

Keep not back: bring my sons from far, and my daughters from the ends of the earth;

Even every one that is called by my name: for I have created him for my glory, I have formed him; yea, I have made him.

Isaiah 43:1-7

The Creator of Heaven and Earth told the Levites to put His name upon His chosen people Israel in Numbers 6:24:

"The Priestly Blessing" which says, "May Yahwah Bless Thee and Keep Thee. May Yahwah Cause His Face to Shine Upon Thee and Be Gracious Unto Thee. May Yahwah Lift Up His Countenance Upon Thee and Give Thee Peace."

In this scripture, for instance, the name of the Creator, Yahwah, is itself part of the priestly blessing, rather than the word "God." There are other scriptural references, later in this work, that further illuminate the power of the Creator's name, and the inherent blessing in correctly recognizing, and utilizing it.

Thou shalt not take the name of YAHWAH thy God in vain; for YAHWAH will not hold him guiltless that taketh his name in vain.

Exodus 20:7

A SPIRITUAL BEING VERSUS A PHYSICAL BEING

In the beginning God created the heavens and the earth and the spirit of God hovered over the face of the waters.

Genesis 1:1

The beginning of the Bible introduces God as the Creator/Spirit who brought everything in the universe into existence. It was a Spiritual Being who made the physical world and all the physical things/beings within it. Christians attempted to change the spiritual image of the invisible Creator, into a physical image or being, that they subsequently named, Jesus or Jesus Christ.

There is absolutely no middle ground between Hebrew Scriptures and Greek writing. Neither is there any way to adhere to Israelite Law and accept Christian doctrine at the same time. In other words, it is impossible to comply with instructions to obey God's Law and Christian teachings, which nullifies His Law. In similar fashion it is inconceivable to acknowledge God as the Eternal Invisible Creator and as a mortal man who died approximately at 33 years of age. Yahwah is invisible to human eyes.

And he said, Thou canst not see my face: for there shall no man see me, and live.

Exodus 33:20

No man hath seen God at any time; the only begotten Son, which is in the bosom of the Father, he hath declared him.

John 1:18

Now unto the King eternal, immortal, invisible, the only wise God, be honor and glory forever and ever. Amen. 1st Timothy 1:17, established first in the Holy Scriptures and later reiterated in certain places in the Greek writings, the Creator is alive and exists eternally. He exercises unsurpassed force throughout the universe.

2nd Corinthians 3:3, states that "God is spirit"

> *Forasmuch as ye are manifestly declared to be the epistle of Christ ministered by us, written not with ink, but with the Spirit of the living God; not in tables of stone, but in fleshy tables of the heart.*
>
> ***2nd Corinthians 3:3***

> *God is a Spirit: and they that worship him must worship him in spirit and in truth.*
>
> ***John 4:24***

> *Now the Lord is that Spirit: and where the Spirit of the Lord is, there is liberty.*
>
> *But we all, with open face beholding as in a glass the glory of the Lord, are changed into the same image from glory to glory, even as by the Spirit of the Lord.*

2nd Corinthians 3:17-18 and in Ephesians 2:22, the temple is described as "a place for God to inhabit by Spirit".

> *In whom ye also are builded together for a habitation of God through the Spirit.*
>
> ***Ephesians 2:22***

> *"And God said: Let us make man in our image, after our likeness, and let them have dominion over the fish of the sea, and over the fowl of the air, and over the cattle and over all the earth and over every creeping thing that creepeth upon the earth."*
>
> ***Genesis 1:26***

Christians contend that this precept indicates that Jesus was present before creation. There is however, no basis for this theory. What will bring clarity to this issue however, is to first, answer the question that many people encounter when reading this scripture "who or what is the 'us' Yahwah is addressing.? We can first conclude that Yahwah was not speaking to "man" because He was speaking about ***making*** man. The pronoun "our" indicates that the forces to whom Yahwah was speaking were spirits like Himself. The logical answer then is Yahwah was addressing the Host of Heaven, who are spiritual beings.

The following verse, Genesis Chapter 2:1: *"Thus the heavens and the earth were finished, and all the host of them,"* shows that the host of heaven was created before man. These spiritual and angelic forces, Yah's army, consists of multitudes, which fulfill the will of the Creator. The Hebrew word for " host" (צבאות), means "army." The Host of Heaven mentioned in Genesis 2:1 are angelic forces, which existed before man.

Thus the heavens and the earth were finished, and all the host of them.

Their spirits are higher than man, but are subservient to the Creator. They are spirits with an intellect and they were referred to with the use of the pronoun "us" in the statement, " Let us make man in our image…" Elements in the form of gases and minerals in the atmosphere and the universe could also possibly be included in the realm of the host of Heaven. Many of the minerals, gases and elements are essential parts of man's makeup and are absolutely necessary for human existence.

Man like his Creator was to rule and have dominion over the creatures of the earth. Man in the spiritual image and spiritual likeness of his Creator was to be a creature with intellect, with the ability to think, reason and understand like his Creator. Man functions through intellect, performing conscious mental activities such as thinking, creativity, reasoning, remembering, learning words, imagining and using language. He possesses the spiritual attributes of love, hate, jealousy.

Man like his Creator, and Maker, possesses intellect in the image of Yahwah, which allows him to communicate with his fellow man as well as with Yahwah through speech - something none of the other creatures can do. In this distinct manner, man exist as a spiritual being made in the spiritual image and likeness of his Creator. Yahwah exists as the Supreme in all the above attributes, eternally.

In Genesis 2:7, after the creation of the plants and the herbs of the field did Yah create man. *And the Lord God formed man of the dust of the ground, and breathed into his nostrils the breath of life; and man became a living soul.*

The "breath" of the Creator was literally the Spirit of Yah, confirming the fact that Yahwah is a Spiritual Being who gave life to the physical creation, and to man.

Proverbs 8 states that "Yahwah made wisdom as the beginning of his way, the first of his works of old." Here we see clear evidence that the creation of wisdom was the first act in the process of creation. It was by intellect, knowledge, and understanding the Creator founded the universe. It was a perfect plan with everything having its purpose.

According to Genesis 1:3, *And God said: 'Let there be light'. And there was light* (ואמר יהוה יהי-אור). The first spoken "words" brought forth light, in this case the physical manifestation of the sun, moon and stars as described in Genesis 1:14-18

> *And let them be for lights in the firmament of the heaven to give light upon the earth: and it was so.*
>
> *And God made two great lights; the greater light to rule the day, and the lesser light to rule the night: he made the stars also.*
>
> *And God set them in the firmament of the heaven to give light upon the earth,*

And to rule over the day and over the night, and to divide the light from the darkness: and God saw that it was good.

From the beginning, we can see the divine order of the creative process: Yahwah's will, being manifested first in the creation of wisdom, following through to the rest of the physical creation, culminating with the creation of man, and the infusion of Yah's breath within him.

Yet it is here, within this foundational creative story, that Christians begin the erroneous attempt of validating the existence of Jesus. Why here? The reasons are logical and very basic; by injecting him into the creative story at the onset, Jesus would then be validated by Old Testament teachings, ultimately placing him in the beginning of creation, and, according to their logic, prove that he is God himself.

The book of John contains several key precepts that Christians use in order to tie Jesus, into the Genesis story.

"In the beginning was the Word, and the Word was with God, and the Word was God."

John 1:1

"And the word was made flesh, and dwelt among us, and we beheld his glory as of the only son of the Father full of grace and truth."

John 1:14

John 1:14, is a precept which not only contradicts the truth in the Old Testament, but also strays from its hebraic principles. As we have just seen, in the Old Testament, Yahwah is Spirit - the definitive creative spirit - unseen but clearly evident through the various manifestations of Yahwah's will, which we understand as man and the surrounding creation. This invisible Spirit uttered the Word, Yahwah's will, through sound vibrations, which brought all things into existence. The Word existed with the Creator, but it was not the Creator. The Creation, did not exist with God, it came into existence after God. The difference might seem subtle, but is important to note, nonetheless. The "word was made flesh" can only be correct if that "flesh" is a euphemism for the collective creation that the Holy record goes on to describe. It cannot, and should not be miscontrued to point to the existence of Jesus Christ, as Christians attempt to indicate. Again, a subtle difference, in this instance turning on a single word, but the ramifications as a result of a grave misunderstanding, are too much to ignore.

It is important to note, that not all Christians support the views expressed here. However, I am mentioning these positions because they have been the most prevalent in the many conversations I have had with Christians world-wide.

Christians make another attempt to inject Jesus in the events that took place in the Garden of Eden story in Genesis 3:-15. Several precepts in the chapter 3 refer to the "seed" of the union between Adam and Eve. Many Christians interpret this seed as a reference to the future coming of Jesus. When in fact, that seed that results from Adam and Eve's union, refers both to a spiritual character that would also identify a particular people. In verse 15, the Creator is addressing the evil force in the Garden of Eden, who is called Nacosh.

> *And I will put enmity between thee and the woman, and between thy seed and her seed; it shall bruise thy head, and thou shalt bruise his heel.*

In verse15, the Creator is addressing the evil force in the Garden of Eden, who is called Nacosh (נחש), which indicates a being who has been cast down to the earth. Although, this spirit manifested itself in human form, it is classified as a beast.

Initially, Adam was questioned concerning the sin which had taken place. Adam blamed Eve, his help-meet, which Yah had given him, and Eve blamed the serpent (nacosh) for her act, in like manner, as she was interrogated by Yah. Yet there was no need to question the "nacosh" or the "serpent" because, Yah knew that the serpent was the only creature in the Garden, with the knowledge of good and evil. The mission of this subtle upright beast was to use the woman as his vehicle to reproduce his seed in the earth. The Creator counters his plan with the reprimand that there would be enmity or hatred between their offspring, the offspring of Adam and Eve's union (the Sons of Light), and that of Eve's union with the serpent/nacosh.. The seed of Adam was designated as Sons of Light or Good, and the seed of the adversary, nacosh, the "serpent" or satan, were henceforth referred to as the sons of darkness, or evil.

Christianity makes another attempt to tie Jesus into the Old Testament with Genesis 22:8. It is interesting to note that these claims are made from simply reading the precepts starting in the middle of the passage. Yet that particular passage concerning Abraham, can only be fully and rightly understood, when read from the beginning. The context of this passage concerning Abraham in itself shows that a ram was caught in the thicket and does not refer to Jesus. The proof is in the entire reading and comprehension of the passage in Genesis 22:1-8:

And it came to pass after these things, that Yahwah did prove Abraham, and said unto him "Abraham; and he said, "here Am I. And he said: "take now thy son, thine only son, whom thou lovest, and get thee into the land of Moriah; and offer him there for a burnt-offering upon one of the mountains which I will tell thee of. And Abraham rose early in the morning, and saddled his ass, and took two of his young men with him, and Issac his son; and he cleaved the wood for the burnt-offering, and rose up, and went unto the place of which Yahwah had told him. On the third day Abraham lifted up his eyes, and saw the place afar off. And Abraham said unto his young men: Abide ye here with the ass, and the lad and I will go yonder, and we will worship, and come back to you. And Abraham took the wood of the burnt offering and laid it upon Isaac his son; and he took in his hand the fire and the knife; and they went both of them together. And Isaac spoke unto Abraham his father and said: "My Father and he said: Behold the fire and the wood; but where is the lamb for a burnt-offering? And Abraham said, "Yahwah God will provide himself the lamb for a burnt-offering, my son.

Indeed, all happened accordingly. In Genesis chapter 22:2, Yahwah tests the loyalty of Abraham by requesting that he take Isaac to mount Moriah for a **burnt offering** sacrifice. In verse 7, Isaac who is an adolescent and quite aware of the objects used for sacrifice, inquires about the lamb, which is missing at this particular time. In verse 8, Abraham unable to speak his natural mind says to Isaac, "Yahwah will provide for himself a burnt offering." At that very moment Abraham's intention was to offer Isaac as a burnt offering. However, Yah literally provided the ram as the offering instead. It is the entire chapter which certainly reveals the obvious facts. Christians attempt to put a metaphysical spin on what is a literal understanding, as a convenience to satisfy a falsehood. This is unacceptable.

This chapter of Genesis clearly deals with the Israelite patriarch Abraham whom the Creator had previously called from Ur of the Chaldees and promised to make him the father of a multitude of nations. Abraham was also told to sojourn in the Promised Land of Canaan which would be given to Abraham's descendants as an everlasting possession.

Genesis Chapter 22, Verses 9-13 continues, *they came to the place which Yahwah had told him of and Abraham built the altar there, and laid the wood in order, and bound Isaac his son, and laid him on the altar, upon the wood. And Abraham stretched forth his hand, and took the knife to slay his son. And the angel of Yahwah called unto him out of heaven, and said: " Abraham, Abraham, and he said: "Here Am I" and he said: Lay not thy hand upon the lad, neither do thou anything unto him, for now I know that thou art a God-fearing man, seeing thou hast not withheld thy son, thine only son, from Me. And Abraham lifted up his eyes and looked and behold behind him a ram caught in the thicket by his horns. And Abraham went and took the ram, and offered him up for a burnt offering instead of his son.*

Just imagine, based on the line which states, a ram was caught in the thicket by his horns, Christian doctrine without any contextual logic attempts to force Jesus in the understanding of the Old Testament precept.

Nowhere in the entire Old Testament is there a single instance of the accepting a human sacrifice. In fact, the Creator condemns and abhors foreign nations who sacrifice their children to false gods.

The providing of the ram, by Yah, and its subsequent sacrifice were literal acts, that were part of the test of Abraham's faith. The context of the thoughts in Genesis chapter 22, verses 13-19 concludes this particular episode in the life of the Patriarch Abraham. It has nothing to do with Jesus or Christianity. It reads:

> *And Abraham lifted up his eyes, and looked, and behold behind him a ram caught in a thicket by his horns: and Abraham went and took the ram, and offered him up for a burnt offering in the stead of his son.*
>
> *And Abraham called the name of that place Jehovah-jireh: as it is said to this day, In the mount of the Lord it shall be seen.*
>
> *And the angel of the Lord called unto Abraham out of heaven the second time,*
>
> *And said, By myself have I sworn, saith the Lord, for because thou hast done this thing, and hast not withheld thy son, thine only son:*
>
> *That in blessing I will bless thee, and in multiplying I will multiply thy seed as the stars of the heaven, and as the sand which is upon the sea shore; and thy seed shall possess the gate of his enemies; And in thy seed shall all the nations of the earth be blessed; because thou hast obeyed my voice. So Abraham returned unto his young men, and they rose up and went together to Beer-sheba; and Abraham dwelt at Beer-sheba.*

Death and destruction is prophesized against the inhabitants of the earth in our day, in the Bible. The Creator also has a controversy with Israel in our day, in the Bible. We have yet to acknowledge Him as a people like most of mankind. The Power who created this earth and universe is a jealous Power. The age in which we find ourselves is designated by the Creator to reveal himself and destroy all who deny his omnipotence.

Numbers 23:19, I Samuel 15: 28-31 and Hosea 11:7-9. Each of these precepts emphatically state that GOD is <u>not</u> a man.

> *God is not a man, that he should lie; neither the son of man, that he should repent: hath he said, and shall he not do it? or hath he spoken, and shall he not make it good?*
>
> ***Numbers 23:19***
>
> *And Samuel said unto him, The Lord hath rent the kingdom of Israel from thee this day, and hath given it to a neighbor of thine, that is better than thou.*
>
> *And also the Strength of Israel will not lie nor repent: for he is not a man, that he should repent.*
>
> *Then he said, I have sinned: yet honor me now, I pray thee, before the elders of my people, and before Israel, and turn again with me, that I may worship the Lord thy God.*
>
> *So Samuel turned again after Saul; and Saul worshiped the Lord.*
>
> ***I Samuel 15: 28-31***
>
> *And my people are bent to backsliding from me: though they called them to the most High, none at all would exalt him.*
>
> *How shall I give thee up, Ephraim? how shall I deliver thee, Israel? how shall I make thee as Admah? how shall I set thee as Zeboim? mine heart is turned within me, my repentings are kindled together.*

I will not execute the fierceness of mine anger, I will not return to destroy Ephraim: for I am God, and not man; the Holy One in the midst of thee:

Hosea 11:7-9

The Holy Scriptures are explicit in their declaration that the Creator is a Spirit and not a physical being. The precepts above tell us plainly the Creator is not a man. Therefore any effort to make Jesus the Creator is baseless. The concept that Yah is a physical being is not supported anywhere in the Old Testament. Furthermore, we are also told in Deuteronomy 4:13-20, that we must not make any graven image of the Creator, the likeness of any figure in heaven, earth or the waters beneath the earth.

And he declared unto you his covenant, which he commanded you to perform, even ten commandments; and he wrote them upon two tables of stone.

And the LORD commanded me at that time to teach you statutes and judgments, that ye might do them in the land whither ye go over to possess it.

Take ye therefore good heed unto yourselves; for ye saw no manner of similitude on the day that the LORD spake unto you in Horeb out of the midst of the fire:

Lest ye corrupt yourselves, and make you a graven image, the similitude of any figure, the likeness of male or female, The likeness of any beast that is on the earth, the likeness of any winged fowl that flieth in the air, The likeness of any thing that creepeth on the ground, the likeness of any fish that is in the waters beneath the earth:

And lest thou lift up thine eyes unto heaven, and when thou seest the sun, and the moon, and the stars, even all the host of heaven, shouldest be driven to worship them, and serve them, which the LORD thy God hath divided unto all nations under the whole heaven.

But the LORD hath taken you, and brought you forth out of the iron furnace, even out of Egypt, to be unto him a people of inheritance, as ye are this day.

Deuteronomy 4:13-20

Man knows of no other realm outside of heaven, earth and in waters beneath the earth. Therefore, we must not make any physical image or mental image of Yahwah our creator.

For I am the LORD, I change not; therefore ye sons of Jacob are not consumed.

Malachi 3:6

THE RACE ISSUE IN THE SO-CALLED BIBLE

"Anyone who wants to understand the Scriptures must realize the fact that the Bible contains the history of a particular people with a definite nationality, the Nation of Israel or "Yisrael." This statement was made by the late leader of the Worldwide Church of God, Herbert W. Armstrong.

Mr. Armstrong a devout Christian, went on to say "it is undeniable! It's history, from Genesis to Revelation is primarily the history of one nation of people – the Israelites. Other nations are mentioned only in so far as they came into contact with Israel. All its prophecies also pertain primarily to this people, Israel. The Old Testament tells of these Israelites and their God." The God of Abraham, Isaac and Jacob, is seen exclusively in the inspired writings of the Israelites.

Mr. Armstrong, taught that the British and Americans are the descendants of Israelites and indicates this in his book, "The United States and Britain in Prophecy." Mr. Armstrong's twist on this matter is consistent with other Christian distortions concerning the Holy Scriptures. As a result, there is wide spread confusion and misunderstanding. Inadvertently, Christians have missed the facts and believe the New Testament was written by Israelites. This deception is a major reason for strong, but wrong beliefs. Statements recorded in the New Testament play a major role in the deception and confusion held by many Christians. Many sincere Christians believe that the entire so-called Bible is truth. They believe the Bible is one consistent word of God. One could not be further from the Truth.

The first New Testament was written hundreds of years after the tribes of Israel were taken into captivity among the nations. All prophecy and Divine contact with their God had ceased. Someone other than Israelites wrote the New Testament writings.

To suggest that the Hebrew Israelites who were promised an enslavement marked by a physical, mental and spiritual confusion compounded with worldwide dispersion and Divine abandonment was modified by God in the New Testament is ridiculous. To think that the God of Israel had reversed His decree against them spoken emphatically by the Prophets is a gross distortion of the Truth. The chronology of the captivity and punishment runs simultaneously with the New Testament period and beyond. Christians believe that the Israelites ceased to prophesize in their own Hebrew language and began to do so in the Greek language. However, most of the New Testament writers and characters are thought to be fictitious by many scholars. There are just too many unknown characters or indecisive individuals with first names only. These alleged people exist without any actual record or proof of even a surname. A great deal is assumed about Christian doctrines, very little is known about the facts.

Among many Christians, genealogy and nationality no longer have any bearing. Yet not all branches of Christianity agree on their significance. Quite often when Black Christians hear other Blacks declare that they are descendants of Ancient Israel, a spirit of disgust arises. Why put racism in religion? More often than not, Black Christians believe it is racist to view the characters or people of the Bible by any color other than White - a testimony to the almost complete brainwashing done to them by Christian theology. To go against this accepted norm is racist and wrong, regardless that it has been done consistently over the centuries by White Christians.

On the other hand, Black and White Christians alike find virtually nothing wrong with Eurpoeans portrayal or claims to Israelite connections in the Bible, regardless of how spurious, illogical or absurd. It seems as though, ideas which meet that status quo, are readily accepted as true. It's important to remember the old adage, "What is popular is not always true and what is true is not always popular."

European Jews have claimed to be the people of the Bible for a long time. But, mounting evidence to the contrary has cast doubt on many minds as to the validity of their claim. Thousands of black Israelites across the globe are increasing their awareness of their bonafide ancestral connection to the Biblical Patriarchs, Abraham, Isaac and Jacob.

"For the purpose of clarification, it must be stated here, that although some writers and scholars attempt to use the names of Israel and Jew, interchangeably, the name Israel, itself is the appropriate identification of the ancient nation or people. The terms are in no way synonymous."

Israelites and Jews -The Significant Difference
Cohane Michael Ben-Levi

Herbert W. Armstrong and other European teachers taught their Christian followers that Britains and Americans were the seed of Israel. As Armstrong writes and others concur "the so-called Bible is an Israelite book, pre-eminently of and for the Israelite nationality, inspired by God through their Prophets. Is it not indeed strange that we English speaking peoples are today the greatest believers in and exponents of this book of the Hebrew people; that of all nations, we are the chief worshippers of Israel's God and Israel's Messiah-in name and in form, if not in Truth and deed."

Isn't that interesting? If not in truth and deed, then how? The statement that Europeans are chief worshippers of Israel's God is not accurate because Jesus is neither the God of Israel nor their Messiah. The word Messiah pertains specifically to an anointed king or high priest of Israel. The irony is that English speaking peoples are today's greatest proponents of what was essentially an historic document that spoke almost exclusively of the Hebrew people, their doctrine and culture, yet their own practice of it, reflects neither the correct history, culture or even the correct ethnicity of the people themselves. Some Europeans have even suggested that portions of Israel are "lost", while others have even gone as far as to say that Israel has been eradicated completely. Either position seems designed to allow them to pose as Israel "in-absentia."

Think. Let us be intelligent and acknowledge that the people of Israel have to be somewhere on the planet earth today. Israel is an ethnic group, a nation, not a religion. Israelites have nothing to do with religion or religious teachings. The Bible history occurs in the geographical region which, encompasses the Eastern hemisphere, inclusive of Africa and Asia. The central territory is called the Fertile Crescent which is far from Europe. Biblical characters were people of Shemitic and Hamitic language groups. There is absolutely no such thing as "spiritual Israel" - another group of people who somehow inherited Israel's legacy and promises from the Creator, (in many instances Europeans) according to some Christian teachings. Israel is Israel - past, present and future.

If we were to use to today's definitions of ethnicity, we would say that they are what is now known as Black Africans, or people of African descent. There are a number of excellent books that delve into this subject much more deeply, including; ***Hebrewisms of West Africa*** by Joseph J. Williams; ***God the Black Man and Truth*** by Ben Ammi; and my own earlier work, ***Israelites and Jews - the Significant Difference***.

The Eastern world is a place made up of people of color past and present. The occidental presence in the Old Testament is very limited. The use of the word color in this text will not trivialize the issue with a Black or White rhetorical comparison. The reference to race is to point-out the facts which shows a deliberate manipulation of the physical characteristics by Europeans who changed physical features, and portraits of the people from Black to White.

Race has been made a closed issue, but the controversy of race is an open issue in the Bible. The race issue has been a major battle waged by religious forces. Yet, the ever emerging Truth is rising. The message in this book cannot be the words of a hate-filled individual whose anger has blinded him to the point where he has become a racist. It is built on scholarship rather than rhetoric.

Sometimes, the very thing which we thought was the farthest thing from the Truth, is theTruth. At times, the idea ruled out without question or without investigation is the very place where the truth exists.

Millions of people read the Bible daily and they form interpretations to suit their religious doctrine. The fact remains that the people Divinely planted by the Creator through the lineage of Abraham, Isaac, and Jacob are still dispersed among the nations of the earth.

Christianity says that the ancient Israelites no longer exist and the Laws given to them by the Creator have been done away with and no longer apply. They have placed their own spin on the prophecies in the Old Testament. It is impossible to undermine the Almighty. No matter how many deceptions have been created or how many veils have been placed over the truth, ultimately the truth will be unveiled.

The false recognition of true Israel is a single miscalculation. This perhaps is the most important factor behind their failure to understand the Holy Scriptures. They have not been taught that the Blacks are the true Israelites. By not realizing that the seed of Israel is still alive in the earth in great numbers living under the affliction and oppression through captive enslavement, Christians fail to realize many other essential facts recorded in the Old Testament. Even worse, is the fact that they are rejecting and challenging the Almighty. There is only one expectation to the issue of Israel according to prophesy, Israel will be regathered and restored as the Kingdom of Yah and its Laws will become the teaching and light for the nations of the earth.

> *Therefore, behold, the days come, saith the Lord, that it shall no more be said, The Lord liveth, that brought up the children of Israel out of the land of Egypt;*
>
> *But, The Lord liveth, that brought up the children of Israel from the land of the north, and from all the lands whither he had driven them: and I will bring them again into their land that I gave unto their fathers. Behold, I will send for many fishers, saith the Lord, and they shall fish them; and after will I send for many hunters, and they shall hunt them from every mountain, and from every hill, and out of the holes of the rocks.*
>
> ***Jeremiah 16:14-16***

Consequently all nations will know God, understand and therefore, acknowledge, serve and obey the One Creator, the only true power.

THE TRUE ISRAELITES IS DNA THE ANSWER?

"Shroud of Turin has human DNA" is a headline, that appeared in the New York Daily News on Sunday, March 29, 1998. The article was written by the Daily News staff writer, Marcus Baram.

This article is one of hundreds filled with obscure information about Jesus and the alleged events of the 1st Century recorded in the New Testament.

"Scientists in Texas, say they have isolated DNA recovered from the Shroud of Turin, the cloth that some believed Jesus was wrapped in, after being brought down from the cross.

Tests, by Victor Tryon, Director of the Center for Advanced DNA Technologies at the University of Texas, turned up traces of DNA in the minute samples of blood remnants.

"The samples are so small and damaged, however, that any DNA in them is practically unusable," says Leoncio Gorza-Valdes, a microbiologist at the University of Texas.

"What we have discovered is that the remnant of human blood, that it is a male," says Gorza Valdez. If they were provided with more samples, the scientist says, "they could uncover further information." You could know the race and part of Israel that they were from, based upon the micro-satellites that the blood has" he says. But the Catholic Church is not cooperating. Arguing that such experimentation is sacrilegious. Turin's Giobanni Cardinal Saldorin, the Pope's official custodian of the shroud, is not releasing more samples and has even recalled the samples that Gorza-Valdes has. In those samples there is not enough material to determine parentage, for example, says shroud expert Father Ian Wilson, and still less for making science fiction-type "clone" of Jesus. Wilson's new book, "The Blood and the Shroud", re-examins the identity of the shroud based on the testing being done at the University of Texas. Combined with other scientific studies, Wilson provides dramatic evidence the cloth dates to biblical times.

In 1988, Italian scientists performed carbon-dating tests on the shroud that showed the cloth dated to the early 1300s more than 1,000 years after Jesus' death. Garza-Valdes and his colleagues discovered that the carbon-dating methods were skewed because the samples were covered with bacteria and fungi. This contamination resulted in the microbes being dated to the 1300s not the actual cloth or the dried blood it contains.

"The amount of contaminant is enough to conclude that it may date from the 1st century," Garza-Valdes says. He thinks that blood traces of the stigmata, cruxcifixion wounds on the hands and feets, clearly indicate Jesus' presence.

"Not many people in the 1st century suffered these lesions, the crown of thorns, the spear wound in the right side of the chest, the flagellating - all of that was unusual for that time. The only historical figure that has received these stigmata is Jesus of Nazareth," he told the Daily News.

Last spring, researchers uncovered more powerful evidence, such as pollen grains removed from the shroud that matched plants indigenous to Israel. Images of flowers adorned the shroud, and those species that grew in the area surrounding, Jerusalem, the site of Jesus crucifixion.

"Until the Church releases the samples, which can be purified of these contaminants, we'll have to wait before we can do more extensive testing," say Prof. Stephen Mattingly, the head of Microbiology at the University of Texas. The Church's reaction is baffling to the scientists. Mattingly, thinks the Vatican doesn't know how to deal with the results of the testing. "I'm sure they are freaked out about what will be revealed – the nationality and race of the figure, that's threatening," he says.

Joseph Zwilling, a spokesman for the Archdiocese of New York, says, "The faith the shroud has inspired, is going to transcend whatever scientific testing proves or disproves." The idea of ever cloning Jesus' remains beyond Zwilling's comprehension.

"I don't think its right, and I hope it never comes to pass," he says. The shroud will go on public display—the third time in this century—from April 18 to June 14th in Turin.

It is obvious, there are people in the highest religious and educational circles involved in the search for sure answers to questions surrounding the identity and existence of Jesus. The content of the discussion in the article points to the fact that many important questions about Jesus remain unanswered in spite of the accounts written by Matthew, Mark, Luke and John in the New Testament, the most authoritative historical annals on the period.

The quotation of Professor Stephen Mattingly, indicates that there is deep suspicion that Catholic Church officials in the Vatican are concerned about opening a can of worms which could reveal issues crucial to the maintenance of hidden facts on the Christian religion.

The scientific studies and other types of historical, investigative research and analysis are becoming an ever-increasing anxiety for many Christians. Some Doubting Thomases have always existed among Christian folds worldwide. It is clear, that the unfolding of the facts will confirm or refute their doubts once and for all.

Unfortunately, the triumph of truth and justice for the sake of God's glory will not be considerate or sensitive to the emotions of doubters or anyone else. The idea of cloning Jesus or any human being is indicative of just how far man has attempted to challenge or compete with the power of God. It shows how ludicrous the idea of Jesus being God truly is. With a little stretch of our imagination, if man were to clone Jesus and if Jesus is God, then it would mean that cloning Jesus would make man the Creator of God, rather than God being man's Creator. This logic would ultimately render everything in the Bible, baseless.

The deification of man goes back to the earliest kingdoms of ancient times. Egyptian, Babylonian and Assyrian Empires which predates the Greek and Roman empires all had religions based upon virgin birth myths. The rate of men and women becoming gods and goddesses has reached an all-time high in our current age. Of course, most became gods after death, only a handful seem to achieve "divinitiy" while they are still living.

When the vast confusion concerning the truth of Yah is taken into consideration, no one can doubt that there is a need for Yah. Whomever He is, there is a need to establish His Name, Authority and Power in the midst of the earth. And, He will.

It is inconceivable that any Bible reader could believe that the prophecies of the future could be manifested without the gathering and restoration of the true people of Israel.

The True identity of Israel, the people recorded in the Bible has been a greater mystery to the world than any other unknown fact about the Bible. The True nationality or ethnicity of the original peoples is fundamentally as important as the proof that Jesus is supposedly an individual of the nation.

There is an abundance of historical evidence which suggests that the people taken from West Africa and brought to the western Hemisphere in the middle passage or the Atlantic Slave Trade, lie in the Hebrew stock which traces back to the ancestry of Israel. " God, the Black Man and Truth" by Ben Ammi and "Israelites and Jews: the Significant Difference" by Cohen Michael B. Levi, are books written concerning this subject.

A study of blood DNA in millions of Blacks might prove less complicated and more plausible, than the DNA testing of blood remains on a questionable shroud nearly 2,000 years ago. The book of Ecclesiastes written by Solomon says, "A living dog is greater than a dead lion." Why not conduct a study or test of blood DNA samples from the millions of "unidentified" Blacks throughout the world in conjunction with a study of blood DNA from any bonafide Israelite in the world.

All living things are built of cells. Cells are made up of protoplasm. The outer boundary of cell is called the cell membrane. Inside the cell membrane is the jelly like material called cytoplasm, imbedded in the Cytoplasm is the nucleus. The nucleus is the most important part of the cell. Inside each nucleus of most human cells is forty-six chromosomes divided into smaller parts, called genes. Both genes and chromosomes, contain DNA, a chemical compound that the stores hereditary information. The characteristics that appear in us are a result of the dominant and recessive genes we inherited from our parents.

DNA material such as blood or bone matter will yield particular patterns, which can be analyzed by scientists for identification purposes of ethnic groups or individual verification. There are two primary sources which can become the modes for a comparative DNA study of ancient Israelites: DNA of body remains, known to be in ancient graves located in the Holy Land; and DNA should be made from samples of Falasha or Israelites who have resided within Ethiopia for nearly 3,000 years.

A further study of DNA of slaves brought to the Americas and West Indies should follow. An international study, should be comprised of communities among Yoruba, Ebo, the Ashanti of Ghana, all of West Africa, the Zulu of South Africa and elsewhere, to determine the true connection to ancient Israel's roots.

Further research could possibly reveal the tribes of Israel. Each of the twelve tribes should yield a specific DNA blood type. Imagine the scientific breakthrough and impact on the world if the DNA analysis from this study could possibly identify Reubenites, Simeonites, Levites, Judaens, Danites, Josephites (Manasseh, Ephraim) Benjamites Asherites, Gadites, Naphtalites, Zuvulonites, Issacharites anywhere in the world. Imagine the impact on our present Bible understanding and the viewpoints held among religious groups. Indeed, the hypothesis that the Blacks are really descendants of the Israelite people in the Bible is more valid than a theory that Jesus was a descendant. Obviously, we know that millions of unknown Blacks exist. However, the existence of Jesus is yet to be proven.

The Bible mystery concerning the scattering as well as the gathering of true Israel would result into an investigation and evaluation, which would have a shocking effect on the European Judaic and Christian world. There is no doubt it would become the most exhilarating experience for so-called Black people throughout the world.

DNA study as a means of identifying the true descendants of Israelite tribes in the Bible was done over a year ago. The New York Times published a front page article, " DNA Backs A Tribe's Tradition Of Early Descent From The Jews" based on a DNA study of the Lemba Tribe in South Africa. A subsequent program regarding the study was aired on Public Television. The cat, it would seem, has been let out of the bag. What once was hidden or even hushed up, now threatens to be inarguably revealed, by the highest science, in the highest circles. Finally, it would seem, the truth about the People of the Bible, the majority of Blacks across the globe, will be known and acknowledged.

The Old Testament was written over five hundred years (500) before the New Testament was a completed text. Many books in the Old Testament were written as much as a thousand years and upwards, before any writings of the New Testament came into existence. Without the Old Testament the New Testament would not have a leg to stand on. There would literally be no basis for its existence. The New Testament was deliberately placed beside the Old Testament, to form a Bible in order to give it credibility.

Whenever a person reads the Bible, it must be understood that you are reading a history book. There is no place for any theological viewpoint. The subject matter of the Holy Scriptures has nothing to do with the New Testament, nor is there a connection with religion. Yet, to most of the people who have accepted the Christian faith, the exact opposite is the manner in which they have been taught to view the Bible.

All the prophets and spiritual leaders in the Old Testament were Hebrews and of the nation of Israel. In Deuteronomy 12:32, Israelites were instructed not to add or diminish from the word or Law, of YAHWAH. *What thing soever I command you, observe to do it: thou shalt not add thereto, nor diminish from it.* The teachings in the New Testament are guilty of both. In Deuteronomy 18:15-22, *The Lord thy God will raise up unto thee a Prophet from the midst of thee, of thy brethren, like unto me; unto him ye shall hearken; According to all that thou desiredst of the Lord thy God in Horeb in the day of the assembly, saying, Let me not hear again the voice of the Lord my*

God, neither let me see this great fire any more, that I die not. And the Lord said unto me, They have well spoken that which they have spoken. I will raise them up a Prophet from among their brethren, like unto thee, and will put my words in his mouth; and he shall speak unto them all that I shall command him. And it shall come to pass, that whosoever will not hearken unto my words which he shall speak in my name, I will require it of him. But the prophet, which shall presume to speak a word in my name, which I have not commanded him to speak, or that shall speak in the name of other gods, even that prophet shall die. And if thou say in thine heart, How shall we know the word which the Lord hath not spoken? When a prophet speaketh in the name of the Lord, if the thing follow not, nor come to pass, that is the thing which the Lord hath not spoken, but the prophet hath spoken it presumptuously: thou shalt not be afraid of him. Moses is told that only his brethen of Israel will become prophets to the nation of Israel. A spiritual message from a foriegn source is not accepted by them. The principles of the CREATOR, which govern how Israel and man is to live on earth have never and will never change. The Laws given to Israel were their national constitution.

The Laws of Yahwah God will become a standard for all people. In Chapter 45 and 66 of Isaiah, the prophet clearly states, that the CREATOR alone would be a refuge and savior for the righteous. Through His power all humanity will bow and swear by his name only. The present world struggle will be resolved by He who created heaven and earth. History has always manifested itself according to the plan and will of YAH.

Too many sincere Christians who love GOD and desire to serve him by living an upright and moral life of good have simply been deceived. They think that love and belief in Jesus Christ is actually synonymous with love of GOD. They truly believe as they have been taught that Jesus is GOD. But Jesus is not GOD ALMIGHTY. Jesus is not the MOST HIGH of the Universe. Jesus is not the CREATOR and MAKER of heaven and earth. To understand that Jesus is not the Creator, but only one of many creatures among all Creation will be the greatest revelation a Christian will ever have. It is a simple step, which will transfer one from falsehood into Truth. Nothing will be lost. You will only derive gain. There will be a time on this earth "when every tongue will swear to YAHWAH and every knee will bend to him alone.

"I was lost, but now I'm found" have been the words spoken by many Negro preachers in Sunday morning or afternoon sermons. Apply this phrase properly into the context of understanding the bible. And yet, many are paid huge salaries for saving the souls of others.

To read the so-called Bible and not be able to identify the people of Israel among, the people of the earth leaves the reader void of witnessing and understanding the Power of YAHWAH in fulfilling the words of the prophets.

Many Black ministers and preachers are totally unaware of the fact that they are descendants of Israelites written about in their own Bibles. Therefore, they remain "lost" even with their espousal to Christianity and the belief that they have been found by belief in Jesus. They stand before congregations as leaders lost in their own minds of confusion which amount to nothing more than "the blind leading the blind."

For all people will walk every one in the name of his God, and we will walk in the name of the YAHWAH our God forever and ever.

HISTORICAL BACKGROUND OF ISRAEL

Christian teachers who have advocated this falsehood condemn themselves and contradict their teachings, from the very writings upon which their doctrine is based.

What could be more contradictory and greater confusion than when a religious teaching opposes its own religious writings, and when the ideas within their religious books, and their practices are nowhere evident, or are in conflict? To complicate matters even more these Greek writings became the religious heritage and doctrine of the Roman Catholic Church.

It is politically unthinkable that Rome would accept a historical record of an account about itself based on the viewpoint of Hebrew writers, who were not present at the time of the events. Neither would it be agreeable to have their history recorded in the Greek language rather than Latin the language of Rome. It is highly unreasonable that Italians would view the New Testament as their history book rather than a religious book. A basic strategy associated with any individual who lies is to accuse the person who is telling the Truth of lying. In fact, it would be in the best interest of the liar that the Truth never be heard. Therefore, the more the Truth can be opposed or discredited the safer and more secure the lie.

For centuries, Christianity has successfully used all these tactics to maintain the status quo of ignorance about the Truth in the Bible. More and more people are being told that the "Old Testament" is a quaint set of ideas beyond its usefulness. The Law is purportedly "done away with" or was just too hard to do. As a result, YAHWAH abolished them and opted for just "belief in Jesus" instead. Another tactic is the "Anti Christ" strategy . This, of course, strikes at any individual who attempts to oppose Christian doctrine by exposing the misrepresentation of Jesus Christ as GOD or the son of GOD. In this cunning manner, Christians are taught that anyone who opposes the lie is a liar.

It is inconceivable that any serious bible reader or student could study the Bible and not recognize the importance of the historical connection within the context of the writings. The Bible is a History Book. Certainly, in the case of the Hebrew scriptures, the Old Testament. The question of whether or not the Greek Scriptures or New Testament is an authentic historical account has been a moot point for centuries.

The Hebrew Scriptures accounts of antiquity have been confirmed and proven.The annuls and relics of many ancient societies and nations verify and support the facts recorded in the Hebrew Scriptures, the Old Testament.

It is extremely important to research the background of these ancient peoples in regards to their geography, political and social elements if one is truly to understand the Bible. More often than not the individual who reads the Bible as a religious document will fail to comprehend the writings correctly. When Christian teachers attempt to force Jesus into the Holy Scriptures or Hebrew Writings as a historical figure, it is usually done in a metaphysical manner and has no credibility in a historical sense.

The religiousity of their Christian doctrine can never properly address, fit or fulfill the prophetic historic nature of the Hebrew Scriptures. Any attempt to force Jesus into the Holy Scriptures is ludicrous. Religions, be it Christianity or otherwise has nothing to do with the Holy Scriptures or Old Testament. To attempt to fit religion into the Holy Scriptures is like trying to put a child's glove on an adult's hand. It just will not fit. No matter how much you try to force it. It will never fit.

Christian doctrine is numinous. History is not. This is why Christian teachers must also attempt to obliterate the history in the Holy Scriptures or Old Testament with the false claim that their doctrine is the "New" and the Holy Scriptures is "Old." Thus, a "New Testament" and an "Old Testament," when in fact, there is only one inspired word of YAH given to and expressed through the Creator's chosen people. The Hebrew Israelites are the source of the inspired writings, the Hebrew Scriptures or Old Testament.

Christianity in it's use of deception has produced manifold religious extremist. In most cases, these are innocent wonderful people who otherwise with the true knowledge of YAH would live meaningful and productive lives.

The Hebrew Scriptures or Old Testament and Greek Scriptures or New Testament represents writings of two different people with different origins and different beliefs. The Hebrew Scriptures can be described as the inspired writings and spoken words of the Creator of the Universe. These writings were revealed to an elect few in the midst of his chosen people Israel. The inspired writings outline the source of where and how the Universe came into existence. It's emphasis is placed upon the earth and its inhabitants while indicating that there is a greater superhuman life form among the spirit beings in Heaven above.Biblical astuteness can never be achieved without a clear understanding of how Bible chronology unfolds.

The narrations of Moses tell us of the creation of earth, it's many creatures and man. It provides us with the genealogy of the first man and woman on the earth, named Adam and Eve. The fall of man happened because of disobedience and sin. It is described in a sequence of events which occurred from Adam to the generation of Noah.

It is apparent that the earliest inhabitants of the human race corrupted themselves through fornication, promiscuity, violence and murder. The decree to blot man from off the face of the earth was reconciled by the grace shown to Noah and his family who were blessed to replenish the earth. Shem, Ham, Japheth were the descendants of Noah who replenished the earth, and spread themselves throughout the world, after the flood.

In the process of time the Creator called Abram from Ur of Chaldees and exalted him to Abraham which means the father of a Multitude of nations. Abraham became the progenitor of the Ishmaelites (Arabs), Edomites (so-called Jews), and Israelites. The Creator chose Abraham's lineage from his wife Sarah, which consisted of Isaac, Isaac's son, Jacob and from there Jacob's twelve sons. His twelve sons were later surnamed Israel because of their father Jacob's name was changed by YAH. The trials and tribulations of Abraham, Isaac and Jacob are presented in the book of Genesis which also concludes with Jacob, his sons and their descendants settlement into Egypt. Ironically, they managed to survive because of Joseph who rose to great prominence after being sold by his brothers into slavery.

The book of Exodus 1:8-14 begins with the acknowledgement of the Israelites increase in population which brought dread among the new Egyptian monarchy. The birth of Moses takes place at a time when a decree is issued to destroy all of the male children among the Israelites. To further oppress the Hebrew people or Israelites, Pharoah creates an edict to take them into bondage as slaves. The Israelites were put under task masters. Their bondage became increasingly rigorous and cruel.

> *Now there arose up a new king over Egypt, which knew not Joseph. And he said unto his people, Behold, the people of the children of Israel are more and mightier than we:*

Come on, let us deal wisely with them; lest they multiply, and it come to pass, that, when there falleth out any war, they join also unto our enemies, and fight against us, and so get them up out of the land.

Therefore they did set over them taskmasters to afflict them with their burdens. And they built for Pharaoh treasure cities, Pithom and Rameses.

But the more they afflicted them, the more they multiplied and grew. And they were grieved because of the children of Israel.

And the Egyptians made the children of Israel to serve with rigor:

And they made their lives bitter with hard bondage, in mortar, and in brick, and in all manner of service in the field: all their service, wherein they made them serve, was with rigor.

Exodus 1:8-14

At the brink of the crisis a deliverer is sent by YAHWAH to Abraham's descendants. The Israelites were freed from captivity and later established as a Holy people in Cannan, The Promised Land which was given as an inheritance to Abraham, Isaac and Israel forever.

Moses was rescued by Pharoah's daughter after being placed in a basket and left to fate as he floated down the Nile River. In a process of time Moses became the deliverer of his people. Moses was raised as an Egyptian ruler. However, he was born of Israelite slave parentage. His Egyptian education provided him with the qualities of a great leader. He possessed compassion for the poor, care for the weak and understanding of organizational skills required to run a nation. The forty (40) years spent in the wilderness was the beginning of the process to reform the Israelites into an independent and Holy people free of the debauchery of Egypt. However, the years in the wilderness prove to be too difficult, a challenge for the majority of adults who were stubborn, rebellious and consequently died before reaching the Promise land. The receiving of the Law as the constitution of Israel and the construction of the Tabernacle can be sited as the greatest successes or accomplishments during this period. The books of Leviticus, Numbers and Deuteronomy contain the history of the Israelites in the wilderness and the laws which were to be kept in the Holy Land.

At the end of the forty (40) years in the wilderness, only two of the original adult males remained alive. All had died except Joshua, the son of Nun and Caleb who were young men at the time of their liberation from Egypt and that survived the ordeal in the wilderness. Moses passed the mantle of leadership to Joshua. Joshua was given the charge by the ALMIGHTY to conquer the Promised Land. The book of Joshua is inundated with the numerous battles he and the Israelites fought against the Canaanites who occupied the land. Joshua's military success was great. Nonetheless, Israel was unable to conquer and destroy all of the Canaanite inhabitants. Those Canaanites who remained in the land became a snare. Death and destruction followed intermittently for a long period of time.

Consequently, at the time of Joshua's death, when most of the twelve tribes had settled in the territories of their inheritance, a period of Israelite disorder ushered in, followed by a strong Canaanite insurgency. The history recorded in the Book of Judges is characterized by the phrase. **"And again the Children if Israel did that which was evil in the sight of YAHWAH ."** It was a time marked or characterized by each person doing what was right in their own eyes. It was also a time of utter confusion and chaos. The book of Judges is studded with various deliveries by Saviors who rescued the Israelite tribes from different oppressors.

Some of those who extricated the Israelite Nation at various times were Ehud, Jephtah, Deborah and Samson to name a few. Samuel seems to have been the last of the Judges who brought this historical period to a close. On the other hand, with the death of the Prophet Samuel begins the establishment of a monarchy in the Nation of Israel.

The first king of this era was Saul, a young man of the tribe of Benjamin. The reign of Saul is described in the book of 1st Samuel. Saul was an inexperienced youth appointed to form a government. The people of Israel had rejected the two sons of Samuel Hophni and Phinchas as leaders and requested that they have a King like the other surrounding nations. It was Saul's fate to obtain the Kingdom. However, his fate as king ended when he was defeated by the Philistines. He lost his kingdom through his disobedience to destroy the Amalekites on the battlefield. As a result, the Creator chose David, the son of Jesse to be king over Israel during Saul's lifetime. The rivalry between Saul and David extended far beyond their personal conflict. In fact, there was war between the tribes of Benyamin and Judah, long after the death of Saul. The dissatisfaction can be witnessed with the cursing of David by Shemi, the Benjamite, during the time of Abshalom's insurrection.The Prophet Elijah and Elisha were the dominant figures as spiritual forces in Israel in the days of the earliest Monarchies. The intrigue and controversy of David's court became characteristic of the behavior associated with the reign of the Kings of Judah and Israel for centuries to follow.

While the book of First and Second Samuel deal primarily with the reign of Saul and David, the Books of First Kings and Second Kings also provide us with some history of their successors. Solomon succeeded David on the throne. Nevertheless, Solomon's ascension to the throne wasn't without challenge. His brother Adonijah conspired to become king even before the death of David. Solomon's own actions only worsened matters. Solomon multiplied wives and violated the Law with marriages to seven hundred wives and three hundred concubines. Not to mention the temples he financed and constructed for some of his wives to their foreign gods.

Ultimately, Solomon's actions led to a split in the kingdom. Jeroboam, the son of Nebat his captain, became his principal challenge and even a greater rival to his son Rehoboam. Rehoboam became the king of Judah, and ruled the southern Kingdom, after the death of Solomon. Jeroboam ruled the northern kingdom of Samaria. The Hebrew Scriptures of this era is interwoven with the visits by the prophets, Isaiah, Jeremiah, Amos, Hosea and others, who brought messages to the Israelite population in specific places and at specific times.

Four short books of the New Testament tell nearly all we know of the life and teachings of Jesus. These books are the gospel according to Matthew, Mark, Luke, John. The word Gospel means good news. The names Matthew, Mark, Luke and John in actually represent unidentified people. No records exist which can determine a particular surname or genealogy, which can distinguish these individuals from others with the same first name.

The Epistles or letters of Paul tell something of Jesus. The history within the bible is difficult to understand in itself, imagine how much more complicated would it be to comprehend and interpret the symbolic language in prophecy. Quite often metaphors and similes are used in passages, therefore proper sequence of events and accurate chronology must be understood.

In American society it is an accepted practice for lawyers to take clear and obvious facts and twist them before a jury to where the new spin on the facts causes the jury to see a clear cut case of guilt as a not guilty verdict. Those who produced Christian doctrine are like lawyers in the American justice system who skillfully take a set of obvious facts and convince the public jury that the facts are something else. They with hold evidence from the jury, which prevents the public from making a clear decision. If a person reads the Bible and is left to understand it based squarely on the facts, the conclusion will be something entirely different than what it would be after someone else has twisted the facts to support Christian doctrine.

In the final analysis, it is absolutely necessary to reverse the process by retracing the steps taken to falsify evidence and change the truth. Just as people can be placed in prison or incarcerated due to falsication of evidence, there are millions of people who have spent their lifetime imprisoned in their minds for the same reason, because of what has taken place in respect to the Bible.

The creator allowed this to happen because Israel rejected the law. The light of the Creator to guide man in the path of life was removed. The downward spiral has continued ever since. The New Testament is a deceptive smokescreen, which has been cleverly sifted with the Truth.

With the restoration of Israel and truth, the Creator is blowing the smokescreen away. We have reached the age where sin has completely corrupted the habitants of the earth. Darkness and gross darkness has covered the people. Even YAHWAH'S chosen people Israel, have strayed from the path of righteousness laid out in the ALMIGHTY'S Written Laws.

> *And the LORD shall scatter you among the nations, and ye shall be left few in number among the heathen, whither the LORD shall lead you.*
>
> *And there ye shall serve gods, the work of men's hands, wood and stone, which neither see, nor hear, nor eat, nor smell.*
>
> *But if from thence thou shalt seek the LORD thy God, thou shalt find him, if thou seek him with all thy heart and with all thy soul.*
>
> *When thou art in tribulation, and all these things are come upon thee, even in the latter days, if thou turn to the LORD thy God, and shalt be obedient unto his voice;*
>
> ***Deuteronomy 4:27-30***

The truth has always existed with YAHWAH. He is revealing truth to His servants, His people the nation of Israel who were put asleep spiritually. In Isaiah 29:9 he states, *"stupefy yourselves and be stupid! Blind yourselves and be blind! Ye that are drunken, but not with wine, That stagger, but not with strong drink. For Yahwah hath poured out upon you the spirit of deep sleep, And hath closed your eyes; The prophets and your heads, the seers, hath He covered.* Today, they are being awakened and the Truth is being restored to them.The awakening and Restoration of YAHWAH'S chosen people Israel, the so-called Negroes, is taking place simultaneously with the return of the truth of YAHWAH, the GOD of the Universe.

In Deuteronomy chapter 30, verses 1-3, it reads; *And it shall come to pass, when all these things are come upon thee, the blessing and the curse, which I have set before thee, and thou shalt bethink thyself among all the nations, whither Yahwah thy GOD hath driven thee, 2 and shalt return unto Yahwah thy GOD and hearken unto HIs voice according to all that I command thee this day, thou and thy children with all thy heart and with all thy soul; That then Yahwah thy GOD will turn thy captivity, and have compassion upon thee, and will return and gather thee from all the peoples, whither Yahwah thy GOD hath scattered thee.*

Great boxers must exercise their skill in boxing to counter punch their opponent. However, for centuries Israelites have been unable to respond, while others have aggressively attacked them. Because, Israelites are YAHWAH'S representatives of truth, they have been forced to be patient and have been witheld from knowing the precise time and means to counter punch their opponent due to their mental enslavement.

> *And it shall come to pass, when ye shall say, Wherefore doeth the LORD our God all these things unto us? then shalt thou answer them, Like as ye have forsaken me, and served strange gods in your land, so shall ye serve strangers in a land that is not yours.*
>
> ***Jeremiah 5:19***

HISTORICAL BACKGROUND OF CHRISTIANITY

The facts in this book challenge those who purport that the alleged life and story of Jesus Christ as recorded in the New Testament is truth and connected through biological historical lines. How does Jesus have Hebrew roots and ties in the Old Testament? There is absolutely no human being, male or female who has been born without a Father and Mother. It is scientifically and biologically impossible. It is also, most importantly, against the Laws of (Nature) Yahwah.

Since the birth of Jesus, the so called "Immaculate Conception," is inconceivable in Nature and by law, it is logical to say that no such person was ever born in the manner spoken of in the gospel of the New Testament. Whatever facts there may have been, we are not in the position to validate those records today. Moreover, the little evidence left to us in the New Testament is originally from the Greek language, the very culture that forcibly supplanted Hebrew culture. As such, the veracity of their claims is suspect. No people would willingly allow their history and culture to be defined for them by their oppressor.

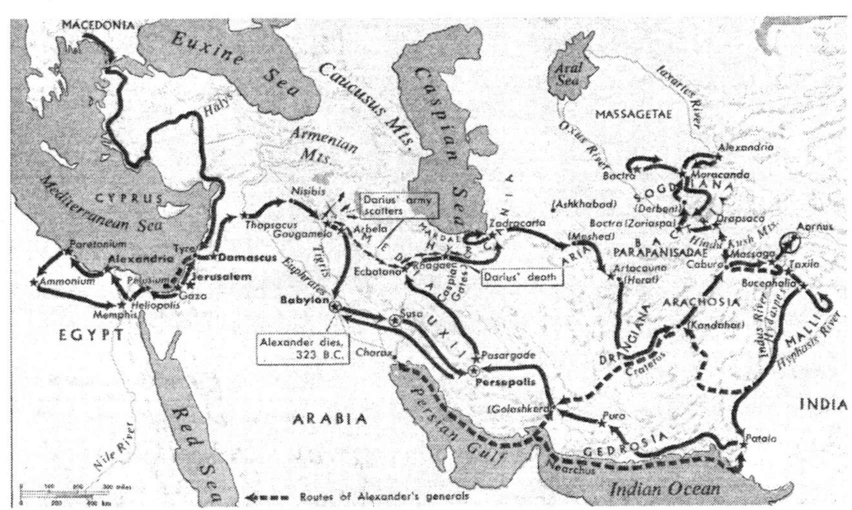

"Euoropean Invasion" Into the Holyland.

The facts represented do not necessarily indicate that there is no more information to present. But, rather that there is no apparent need to do so when there is an abundance of facts that have been already provided to establish the truth. One could literally examine/investigate every sentence and paragraph in the New Testament and find a solid argument in defense of the Truth of the Holy Scriptures (Old Testament) which New Testament and Christian doctrine contradicts.

The Pope is acknowledged worldwide as the Vicar of Christ. In other words, the Pope is believed to be God's representative on earth. Millions of Christians, Catholics in particular, revere the Pontiff as the supreme Christian leader in the world. The Catholic Church is considered to be the Mother of all Christianity from a historical standpoint. The Roman Catholic Church is the founder of the first Christian Church. And today the Vatican in Rome remains the wealthiest of all Christian denominations and still wields considerable political and economic power. Ecclesiastically, however, things have changed.

In the last 600 years, the Catholic church's influence has waned. With the rise of Protestantism and the various sub denominations within it, what were once inarguable tenets of church doctrine, as defined by the Pope, have become increasingly subject to new and different interpretations. There is tremendous division among Christians of various denominations on a wide range of issues concerning the Bible, underscoring the depth of the confusion surrounding Christian doctrine.

An outstanding example of this disagreement is the manner in which Catholics regard "Mary" the alleged mother of Jesus. Among Catholics Mary is given a reverence, which supercedes or at least equals that given to Jesus. This is evident in Catholic ceremonies, which differ greatly from many offshoots of the church that no longer regard Catholicism as the authoritative teaching of the gospels.

There is also a significant difference on the issue of baptism among Christians. Catholics, Protestants and Baptists differ considerably in the manner in which they practice and explain their theories on baptism.

Many Christians continue to disagree as to whether Jesus is God or the Son of God. Furthermore, the trilogy, doctrine of the trinity or union of the three divine persons (father, son, and Holy Spirit or Holy Ghost) in one Godhead is also a divisive topic.

When Christian teachers of various denominations are asked who is actually Jesus' father, answers vary. Some claim Joseph is his father, others say he is the son of God, but an angel is directly responsible for the impregnation of Mary. Some suggest the Angel Gabriel while others declare it was Michael, the Archangel. One thing is certain, there appears to be no single answer to any of these and hundreds of other questions about Christian teachings. Christians have always attempted to explain the unexplainable with supernatural answers - in many cases, the more outlandish, the more accepted. Invariably, the division among Christians on their various interpretations of the Bible stands to highlight the weaknesses in their teachings as a whole.

Protestantism is the religion of Christians who do not belong to the Roman Catholic Church or one of the Eastern Orthodox churches. Protestantism includes hundreds of denominations and sects that differ in varying degrees. About 324 million persons - about one-twelfth of the world's population belong to these various groups.

These explanations of the various denominations of Christianity are listed simply to illustrate the numerous beliefs and contradictions contained within one so-called "belief system." When we examine Protestantism for example, we see how most of these doctrines evolved as a result of someone simply taking an adversarial stance to someone else's interpretation. The fact that none of them, Catholicism included, are grounded in Biblical (Old Testament) truth is glaringly obvious.

Protestantism resulted chiefly from the Reformation, a religious and political movement that began in Europe in 1517. The word Protestant comes from the Latin word Protestants, which means one who Protests. Several German leaders first used it in 1529 as a protest against Roman Catholics attempts to limit the practice of Lutheranism, an early Protestant movement. The term soon came to include all the Western Christians who had left the Roman Catholic Church.

Most Protestant denominations originated during the Reformation. However some, such as the Moravian Church, had been established before the Reformation. The Reformation itself began 1517 when Martin Luther, a German monk, protested certain practices of the Roman Catholic Church. By 1550, Protestantism had spread throughout almost half of Europe.

Protestantism developed as a series of semi-independent religious movements. These movements resembled one another in their rejection of the central authority of the Pope. But, cultural, geographic, political and religious differences caused them to develop independently in varying degrees. Many such differences resulted in the division of a movement into various denominations and sects. Despite their differences, the various protestant movements can be divided historically into five general groups: the conservative Reform Movements; the Radical Reform Movements; the Free Church Movements; the Methodist Movement; the Unity Movement.

The conservative Reform Movements rose during the 1500's. These movements include groups that originally broke away from the Roman Catholic Church but kept many basic beliefs of that church. The Lutheran, the Reformed or Presbyterian, and the Anglican or Episcopalian Church are among such movements.

Huldreich Zwingli and John Calvin developed the teachings of the Reformed or Presbyterian Movement. In 1520, Zwingli a Swiss priest urged reforms that were more radical than Luther's. Calvin's teachings strongly influenced people in England, France, the Netherlands, and Scotland. In England, many of his followers became known as Puritans. In France, they were called Huguenots. It was John Knox who introduced Calvin's teachings to Scotland.

The Anglican or Episcopalian Movement started in England. It was created from the Act of Supremacy of 1534, in which King Henry VIII declared his independence from the Pope. The Anglican Church was established in England only after much dispute and bloodshed. In 1559, Queen Elizabeth I established a moderate form of Protestantism that became known as Anglicanism.

The radical Reform Movement occurred during the 1500's and 1600's. Some small religious sects differed widely from both the Roman Catholic Church and major Protestant churches. Many of these sects rejected conservative reforms and developed their own forms of worship. Included among these sects are Quakers, Separatists and the Shakers.

The Free Church Movements also began in the 1500's and 1600's. This group consisted of the congregational and the Baptists, both of whom developed chiefly from Puritan Churches.

In the early 1600's English clergyman John Smyth led a group of Separatists to the Netherlands. He and his followers believed that only people who were old enough to express their faith should be baptized. Symth's group became known as Baptists.

The Methodist Movement during the 1700's developed largely from pietism, a religious attitude that began in Europe during the late 1600's. Pietism stresses the importance of personal devotion and morality as the true expressions of faith. In the early 1700's, John Wesley, an English clergyman, set out to reform the Anglican Church, also known as the Church of England.

In the 1800's and 1900's the Unity Movement began as a result of many Protestants' and other Christians' increasing desire to overcome their differences. They also worked to increase good will among Protestants and members of the Eastern Orthodox and Roman Catholic Churches.

Methodists belong to Protestant religious denominations that trace their beginnings back to John Wesley. In the United States, many denominations share the name Methodist and a common heritage in Wesley's teaching. The largest Methodist body is the United Methodist church, formed in 1968 through a union of the Methodist church and the Evangelical United Brethren church. Other major denominations include the African Methodist Episcopal Zion Church, the Christian Methodist Episcopal Church and the Free Methodist Church of North America.

Methodist Churches are evangelical. That is, they try to convince non-Methodists of the soundness of the Methodist approach to religion. All Methodists stress salvation through faith, and emphasize an orderly, active Christian life and God's's forgiveness of personal sins. They believe in a personal religious experience in which each individual gives proof of a belief in Jesus Christ as his or her personal savior. Methodists accept the Bible as the Supreme rule of faith and religious practice.

Protestants share certain Christian beliefs with members of the Roman Catholic and Eastern Orthodox churches. For example, Protestants believe there is only one God. Protestant denominations also believe that in God there are three persons who together form the trinity. Protestants disagree with other Christians about the relationship between humanity and God. As a result of this disagreement, certain Protestant beliefs differ from those of other Christians. These beliefs involve the nature of faith and grace and the authority of the Bible.

Protestants oppose the Roman Catholic doctrine on salvation. Catholics believe that people achieve salvation by having faith in God's grace and by their own merit. That is, by doing good works. But Protestants think this belief in human merit makes people too important in their relationship with God. They also believe it demands too much of humanity because people cannot know when they have done enough to please God. Protestants stress the importance of faith and reject the emphasis on good works.

According to Protestants, God is gracious; that is, He is loving and forgiving. He establishes and is responsible for HIS relationship with people. The belief is people are incapable of saving themselves because of their sins. Therefore, they are saved by the grace of God and not by their own merit. Protestants believe this grace of God comes to man through Christ. They regard Christ's death on the cross as a gift of God's grace. But this grace comes to those who have faith, not to those who do good works. Thus, man receives salvation by having faith in God's grace, which comes to him through Christ.

The beliefs of Roman Catholics are based on both the New Testament and the traditions of the Church Fathers. These traditions come from the declarations of church councils and Popes. They also come from short statements called creeds and from longer, formal statements called dogmas. Most Protestants, on the other hand, believe that the Bible should be the only authority for their religion.

Protestants worship one GOD, but various denominations worship him in many different ways. Protestant liturgies (worship services) range from simple, informal meetings to elaborate ceremonies.

Various Protestant denominations disagree about the nature and number of solemn observances called sacraments. But most denominations include at least two sacraments – Baptism and the Last Supper in their worship.

Baptism is a ceremony that represents either the beginning of the Christian life or a sign of a person's faith. Most Protestants connect baptism with gift of faith and grace from God.

The Lord's Supper is a ceremony that reenacts or recalls Christ's words and actions at the Last Supper. Most Protestants believe it represents God's forgiveness of sinners.

John Wesley tried unsuccessfully to find religious satisfaction by closely following the rules of the Church of England. A turning point in his life came in London in 1738, when he said his heart was "strangely warned." Wesley said he discovered that inner peace comes by faith in God's mercy and grace, not through personal efforts alone. Wesley became unwelcome in Anglican Churches because of his evangelistic vigor in preaching and the strict discipline urged on his followers. He and his followers then began to preach wherever people would gather to listen; on streets, in public squares, and in fields. Wesley believed that salvation is free to all people, not just to a select few, and that God's grace is equal to every need. Such a doctrine appealed to many people in England at that time, especially to the poor and oppressed.

As the movement spread, Wesley established what he called the United Societies, in which he used many lay (un-ordained) preachers. Wesley trained, appointed, and supervised the preachers and his doctrine spread mainly because of their devotion and enthusiasm. He organized them into a Methodist conference in 1744. Wesley realized that this growing movement could not continue to work within the framework of the Church of England. Under this guidance, the Untied Societies developed as an independent church. Although Wesley continued as an ordained Anglican clergyman. Wesley sent preachers to America. Philip Embury preached in New York City about 1766. Robert Strawbridge went to Maryland about the same time. Wesley later sent Francis Asbury and Thomas Coke, who became the first American Methodist bishop.

In 1784, about 60 ministers organized the Methodist Episcopal Church in Baltimore. The denomination grew quickly, as traveling preachers called circuit riders carried the Methodist religion to the frontier. In 1828, a group insistimg on more lay representation in church affairs separated and formed the Methodist Protestant Church. Like Methodism in England, this new Church did not have bishops. In 1844, a group left Methodist Episcopal Church, South. This division occurred over the issue of slavery and constitutional powers within the denominations. The Methodist Episcopal Church, the Methodist Protestant Church, and the Methodist Episcopal Church South reunited in 1939 as the Methodist Church. Methodists in Canada organized into the United Church of Canada in 1925. British Methodists, after periods of division, reunited in 1925.

Baptists are members of a large Protestant religious group who reserve baptism for persons who affirm their faith in Jesus Christ as their savior. Baptist are organized in separate conventions or associations. Many of these organizations are linked together in the Baptist World Alliance. About 26 million Baptists in the United States form the largest single Baptist group in the world. The Baptist Movement developed as one wing of English Congregationalism during the early 1600's. These Baptist, like some earlier Christian groups, opposed the baptism of infants. They insisted that baptism should be restricted to believers who are old enough to make their own declaration of faith. Later, in the 1600's Baptists also insisted that baptism should be by immersion (dipping under water), rather than by pouring or sprinkling.

The earliest Baptist leader was John Smyth, a clergyman in the Church of England. About 1607, Smyth went to the Netherlands with those english exiles who later became the pilgrims of New England. While in the Netherlands, Smyth and 36 of the exiles formed a Baptist church. Differences of opinion developed, and 11 members of the new congregation broke away and returned to England to form a church there in 1611. However, major Baptist growth did not occur in England until the Puritan revolution. Most Baptists accepted as their doctrine a slightly modified Westminster confession of faith formulated by the Puritans in the 1640's.

William Carey, an English Baptist who went to India in 1793, was one of the first English-speaking Christian missionaries. American Baptists joined the foreign Missionary Movement in 1812 when Andoniram Judson went to Burma. The missionary effort later spread to Europe and Latin America. As a result of this activity and the movement of British Baptists into Canada, Australia, and New Zealand, most countries today have at least a small Baptist Community. The Soviet Union has an estimated 545,000 Baptists.

In the American colonies, Roger William formed a Baptist Church in Providence, Rhode Island in 1638. Philadelphia later became the major Baptist center in colonial America. During the years, immediately before and after the American Revolution, the number of Baptists increased greatly. By 1800, the Baptists were America's largest Protestant group. The Methodist ranked as the largest denomination for much of the 1800's but the Baptists now form the largest Protestant group in the United States. This results mainly from paid growth in the South since 1900.

About half of the Baptists in the United States are affiliated with the Southern Baptist Convention. The two Black National Baptist groups – the National Baptist Convention in America and the National Baptist Convention, USA., Inc. – form another large segment. A fourth major group, the American Baptist Churches in the USA, is the oldest continuously active Baptist group. The leading Canadian body is the Baptist Federation of Canada.

In the 1900's the Baptists, like most Protestants were divided on matters of theology. Modernists and fundamentalists differed on how best to understand the Bible. The Modernists emphasized studying the Bible historically rather than as the literal word of God. The fundamentalists feared that the authority of scripture, and thus the basis of Christianity, was being undermined by the new Bible study methods and by acceptance of modern scientific theory.

Every branch of Christianity regardless of denomination is guilty of choosing what men have deem is correct to formulate a modified version of rules, which today has become their brand of religion.

In fact, the word **religion** is not mentioned anywhere in the entire Bible. The foundation of Bible teachings and understanding rest in the original Hebrew language. **There is no word for religion.** The very concept of religion did not exist among the Hebrew Israelite people of ancient days. They were given laws in the form of commandments, statutes and judgements by the Creator.

PENTECOSTAL CHURCHES base their faith and practice on certain religious experiences that are recorded in the New Testament. Pentecostal Churches teaches that every Christian should seek to be "filled with the Holy Spirit." The proof of this occurrence comes when the person speaks in tongues; that is, the person will speak in a language that he or she has never learned. The New Testament refers to the disciples' speaking in tongues on the day of Pentecost mentioned in Acts Chapter 2. Pentecostals also believe that they can receive other supernatural gifts. For example, they believe they can be given the ability to prophesy, to heal, and to interpret what is said when someone speaks in an unknown tongue. The New Testament refers to these gifts in 1 Corinthians 13:8-10, 14:1-6.

> *Charity never faileth: but whether there be prophecies, they shall fail; whether there be tongues, they shall cease; whether there be knowledge, it shall vanish away.*
>
> *For we know in part, and we prophesy in part.*
>
> *But when that which is perfect is come, then that which is in part shall be done away.*
>
> ***1 Corinthians 13:8-10***

Follow after charity, and desire spiritual gifts, but rather that ye may prophesy.

For he that speaketh in an unknown tongue speaketh not unto men, but unto God: for no man understandeth him; howbeit in the spirit he speaketh mysteries.

But he that prophesieth speaketh unto men to edification, and exhortation, and comfort.

He that speaketh in an unknown tongue edifieth himself; but he that prophesieth edifieth the church.

I would that ye all spake with tongues, but rather that ye prophesied: for greater is he that prophesieth than he that speaketh, with tongues, except he interpret, that the church may receive edifying.

Now, brethren, if I come unto you speaking with tongues, what shall I profit you, except I shall speak to you either by revelation, or by knowledge, or by prophesying, or by doctrine?

1st Corinthians 14:1-6.

Aside from these distinctive qualities, however, individual Pentecostal denominations do not usually resemble each other. There are more than three dozen Pentecostal groups in the United States alone. They differ radically in size as well as in their interpretations of matters of faith and practice. The Assemblies of God, for example, have more than 86,000 churches with a membership more than 1,100,000. The Fire Baptized Holiness Church has about 40 churches and less than 1,000 members. The congregations control some churches, while others have bishops who will govern.

Pentecostal Churches trace their origins to revivals of tongue speaking that occurred at Bethel Bible College in Topeka, Kansas, in 1901 and at Azusa Street Mission in Los Angeles in 1906. Similar revivals also took place in Great Britain and in Europe, Asia and Latin America during the early 1900's. Since the 1930's, the Pentecostal denominations have grown rapidly. With a worldwide membership estimated at seven million, the Pentecostal are sometimes called Christianity's "Third Force," alongside Roman Catholicism/and traditional Protestantism. Church of God in Christ is a Christian denomination that bases its faith on the doctrines of the apostle's as received on Pentecost (Act; 2:4). Bishop C.H. Mason and others founded the church in 1895. They began preaching that there could be no salvation without holiness. The Baptist church expelled them because of this teaching. Members believed that the Church name was revealed to the bishop in 1897 from a reference in I Thessalonians 2:14 in 1907, a church meeting in Memphis, TN, formed the first General Assembly of the church of GOD in Christ.

> *And when the day of Pentecost was fully come, they were all with one accord in one place.*
>
> *And suddenly there came a sound from heaven as of a rushing mighty wind, and it filled all the house where they were sitting.*
>
> *And there appeared unto them cloven tongues like as of fire, and it sat upon each of them.*
>
> *And they were all filled with the Holy Ghost, and began to speak with other tongues, as the Spirit gave them utterance.*
>
> ***Acts 2:2-4***
>
> *For ye, brethren, became followers of the churches of God which in Judea are in Christ Jesus: for ye also have suffered like things of your own countrymen, even as they have of the Jews.*
>
> ***I Thessalonians 2:14***

The issue of whether the person we have come to know as Jesus, if he were a Hebrew would have been named Yeshua. This is also one of many other controversies surrounding this obscure period of history. In addition to his true ethnicity, is the question of whether Jesus should be depicted as having Black or White features, which also demands investigation and research. The name Jesus is Greek and the name Yeshua, Hebrew. They both mean "savior" in their respective languages.

One thing is certain, that is, Michelangelo, who painted the portraits which have become common representations for Jesus were taken from a random individual selected for this purpose. Michelangelo never saw or painted the actual person known as Jesus. While the name Jesus is only the Greek word for savior and Yeshua is the Hebrew word for savior, neither of these terms can be proof to identify a definite individual mentioned in the genealogy recorded in Matthew, Chapter 1. The name Jesus became a term more representative of an attribute this alleged individual would perform rather than the actual name Jesus. The absence of his surname also suggests this person is a myth based upon the ficticious writings.

The basic facts behind the origin of Christianity can be a shock into reality for a Christian and even more so if that Christian happens to be Black. Most Blacks throughout the Americas and in the Diaspora inherited the Christian religion through their enslavement. Christianity was part and parcel of the institution of slavery. The slaves originally were forbidden to practice the religion of slave owners.

Many plantation owners resisted the idea of Christianizing slaves initially, but the system of "making a slave" became more defined through the philosophy of men like William Lynch. More White slave owners joined the movement to develop strategies for division, self-hatred and distrust among the Black population. As a result, the freedom of Blacks was no longer seen as a threat. The concept of Christianizing "Black savages" brought from Africa was approved by the church leaders as well as justified legally in courtrooms by European advocates of slavery. To make matters worse the so-called Bible was used as the source of justification.This was especially true in the British territories and North America. In the Spanish colonies, the owners were much more tolerant when it came to accepting their slaves in the Catholic Church. In fact, in the Spanish territories, the slaves saw a marked difference in their treatment when it came to civil rights such as marriage and attending church services. Slaves in Spanish colonies were immediately Christianized. On the contrary, in the British colonies the slaves were not allowed to practice Christianity until after their emancipation. In the West Indies in 1838, the British territories brought in missionaries, which used Christianity as a means of preparing slaves for mainstream society.

Margaret Thatcher, the former prime minister of England, stated, " it only takes one generation of a people to forsake their culture and abandon their language and that culture and language will become lost or destroyed." How much more when generations of a people have done so for centuries.

The true roots of the so-called Negroes prior to slavery has been an unsolved mystery for hundreds even thousands of years. Ironically, the evidence has been right in front of their eyes, and yet hidden by their lack of understanding the very so-called Bible they read. The religious teachings, which the slaves received in their colonization and indoctrination at the time of their physical freedom, became "brain chains" which today constitute their mental slavery, as Christians.

In the territories of North America, the West Indies and Africa where Christianity has been the dominant religion of colonial masters, slaves were taught Christianity in order to assimilate them into mainstream society, to be subtly controlled by their former enslavers. The main objective was to create a so-called Black Englishman, a new design of the so-called White prototype.

It has been said that the descendants of slaves who were brought to the western hemisphere now believe in the religion of their enslavers more than the slave masters. Today, in America and throughout regions of the West Indies, Black people's belief and involvement in European holidays such as Christmas, New Years, St. Valentine's Day, and Easter appear to be greater than Europeans themselves. Blacks always seem to be the greatest consumers at these times, they are heavily targeted for these commercial, religious holidays. Blacks earn far less as an ethnic group, but always seem to spend a greater portions of their earnings and remain in higher debts as consumers.

Given the circumstances under which those of African descent have become Christians, they, in particular, unlike their European enslavers, need to investigate the doctrine of Christianity. The fact that they adopted the religion and culture of their enslavers alone is reason enough to search out the truth. Especially, when one considers that Christianity was subtly forced upon them initially and given the manner in which the doctrine was used to subdue and produce a passive attitude towards their enslavers. A good example of this is how slaves were taught to love their enemies and humbly accept their suffering. See Matthew 5:38-39, 43-44

> *Ye have heard that it hath been said, An eye for an eye, and a tooth for a tooth:*
>
> *But I say unto you, That ye resist not evil: but whosoever shall smite thee on thy right cheek, turn to him the other also.*
>
> *Ye have heard that it hath been said, Thou shalt love thy neighbor, and hate thine enemy.*
>
> *But I say unto you, Love your enemies, bless them that curse you, do good to them that hate you, and pray for them which despitefully use you, and persecute you;*

The natural desire for justice, for redress from the terrible conditions enslaved Africans faced, was subtly redirected toward the "pie in the sky" promise of a greater life in heaven after death. "Turn the other cheek" was the Christian slaver's response. According to the New Testament, Christian doctrine, the lot of slaves would be nothing in the face of the greater reward of the "sweet bye and bye."

> *Servants, be subject to your masters with all fear; not only to the good and gentle, but also to the froward.*
>
> *For this is thankworthy, if a man for conscience toward God endure grief, suffering wrongfully.*
>
> *For what glory is it, if, when ye be buffeted for your*

faults, ye shall take it patiently? but if, when ye do well, and suffer for it, ye take it patiently, this is acceptable with God.

For even hereunto were ye called: because Christ also suffered for us, leaving us an example, that ye should follow his steps:

Who did no sin, neither was guile found in his mouth:

Who, when he was reviled, reviled not again; when he suffered, he threatened not; but committed himself to him that judgeth righteously:

Who his own self bare our sins in his own body on the tree, that we, being dead to sins, should live unto righteousness: by whose stripes ye were healed.

I Peter 2:18-24

However, their former understanding of justice, according to Hebraic Law and culture, was quite the opposite. The 21st Chapter of the book of Exodus verses 23-25, reads:

And if any mischief follow, then thou shalt give life for life,

Eye for eye, tooth for tooth, hand for hand, foot for foot,

Burning for burning, wound for wound, stripe for stripe.

This is the moral standard for justice practiced among righteous people and nations on earth today. When the Japanese attacked Pearl Harbor America didn't turn the other cheek. In Korea, Vietnam and the Gulf War against Iraq, where the American interest was threatened they did not advocate "turn the other cheek." If the policy of the Christian nations is to turn the other cheek, why is there a need for military forces? No people or nation defends itself from an aggressor by turning the other cheek as a defensive policy.

Christianity has succeeded in convincing many of African descent, particularly those who are the descendants of the ancient Israelites, that their culture has been abolished. Millions of Blacks across the globe have been falsely taught that their salvation is with those who enslaved them and Christianized them. This is absurd. It is inconceivable that any other people on earth would accept such an idea under similar circumstances. These perverted teachings have confounded them into not thinking like their ancestors. Christianity is one of the most significant factors behind the present state of spiritual confusion among Black people today. From an educational perspective and historical standpoint, Christian doctrine is probably the greatest form of mental slavery perpetuated on Blacks. As a result, Blacks exist with a deficit in their thinking process. The philosophy and psychology used by slave owner, William Lynch, coupled with Christian indoctrination makes it quite easy to understand why even a book like this would be distasteful to the thinking of some Black folk.

As was discussed earlier in this work, there is a rising awareness within the greater African Diaspora, of Blacks' historical/Biblical connection that is quite at odds with the previously accepted European, Christian model. In recent times, it has become quite apparent that many Black preachers and ministers now view the Old Testament in terms of its African/Eastern historical, cultural, and geographical perspective. The struggle within the Black community, to free their minds and unite, is challenged by their spiritual confusion, and lack of understanding their history within the Bible as it had been mispresented. The Old Testament and New Testament as a fused document, create a great misunderstanding even within the knowledgeable Israelite community. The reality of this indicates that this division and misunderstandings must be resolved in order for the Israelite people to unite. This can only be achieved when an earnest and intellectual comparison of the Old Testament versus the New Testament takes place. The questions to be asked and answered are "what are the facts concerning the recordings in the Old Testament?" And "Are there clear contradictions recorded in the New Testament?" We must investigate the clear contradictions recorded in the New Testament. Furthermore, we must find what are the true facts and circumstances, which caused the church to develop the current religious practices and teachings in Christianity and its denominations.

CHRISTIAN DOCTRINE: THE GREAT DECEPTION

Take heed to yourselves, that your heart be not deceived, and ye turn aside, and serve other gods, and worship them;

And then the LORD'S wrath be kindled against you, and he shut up the heaven, that there be no rain, and that the land yield not her fruit; and lest ye perish quickly from off the good land which the LORD giveth you.

Deuteronomy 11:16-17

The chronology of events between the history recorded in the Hebrew Scriptures or Old Testament and the Greek writings or New Testament which Christianity alleges is a continuation, happens to be divided by more than five hundred years. Many of the original Hebrew Israelite concepts changed when the Greek writers began writing their foreign version of the Bible. The Nation of Israel was scattered by the Most High among the ancient world. As oppressed slaves it was virtually impossible for Israel to record the alleged events described in the Greek writings.

Daily News on Sunday, February 22, 1987, **"Minister Asserts the Bible is hoax".** Only a few curious lunch-time pedestrians saw Hudson Marsden, a retired Baptist Minister tape a booklet and a crucifix containing a sliver of stone from Blarney Castle to the great bronze doors of St. Patrick's Cathedral one day last week, too bad. They missed a chance to hear the most awesome, audacious conspiracy theory of all. The theory is that, well, let Marsden tell it.

> "The New Testament, the Church and christianity were all of the creation of the Colpurnius Piso family, who were Roman aristocrats. The New Testament and all

> the characters in it-Jesus, all the Joseph's all the Mary's all the disciples, apostles, Paul and John the Baptist – all fictional." Wait, there's more. The Pisos used the pen name Flavius Joseph and, to safeguard their literary hoax, used complicated codes based on sounds, animal allusions and numbers. They "invented" christianity to establish a rival religion that would dilute the impact of Judaism and more important, to help shore up the power and influence of the Pisos' in laws – the descendants of Herod the Great, rulers of Judea.
>
> As conspiracies go, this one makes Watergate and Kennedy's assassination sound like amateur hour. "I know" says Marsden, who lives in Rochester and operates an organization called the National Ecumenical Bible Research Center. "But the fact is the New Testament is just like a story, Like "Snow White and the Seven Dwarfs."

The details, in a 32-page booklet entitled "Expose the Life of Jesus" are built on a carefully balanced pyramid of real names, numerology, Old Testament interpretations and great leaps in logic. We are not atheistic or agnostic says Marsden. "We are just looking for a scientific basis for the Bible." The genesis of the theory has its roots in a 1967 seminar in Miami, where Marsden met two rabbis another Baptist minister, a Lutheran Minister and Presbyterian minister who shared his misgivings about the origins of Christianity and the authorship of the New Testament. "We started comparing material and ideas," Marsden says. "We found the proof to support our theory, proof beyond a shadow of a doubt." One by one, the others died. Now only Marsden is left and at age 60, he has a history of heart disease. This is what led to his keeping a strange promise – to not die without revealing the theory. Sure, he expects flak. "It does not bother me," Marsden says, "That's why I got an answering machine. People can say whatever they want to the tape. There are numerous important clues in the Hebrew Scriptures which can be used to determine the Truth whenever contradictions occur between the writings in the Holy Scriptures and the Greek writings."

Christian doctrine has even penetrated the minds of many Israelites in the Diaspora. Most Hebrew Israelites who realized they are bonafide descendants of ancient Israel spoken of in the Bible also came from families with former slave backgrounds and Christian indoctrination. Nevertheless, the ability and blessing to unscramble and separate the truth from the lies in the Bible has baffled and escaped even some Israelites, who represent in some cases elements of the Elect of Yah. Consequently, some groups have been called Messianic Hebrew Israelites, denoting their acceptance of Jesus Christ as the Messiah. Even in the midst of European Jewry there have arisen sects known as "Jews for Jesus." Also, an increasing number of Jewish converts turning to Christianity prompted the author Samuel Levine to write a book entitled, You Take Jesus I'll Take God.

According to the New Testament writings, the Jews were people who rejected Jesus. In any case, the writings in the New Testament stated that Jesus was rejected as God, the Son of God and the Messiah. Among Israelites who are knowledgeable of the Hebrew language and who have researched this obscure period of history, there is an awareness that the evidence surrounding what has been written and purported in the New Testament clashes with the facts in the Old Testament.

It has long been claimed that the Bible contradicts itself. More accurate is the claim that the New Testament contradicts the Old Testament. In order for Christianity to be viewed and accepted as valid the religious leaders would have to claim that the Old Testament's teachings are no longer valid. For Christian doctrine to claim the law has been done away with is a contradiction with its own doctrine and, the New Testament. Whenever the Truth and a lies come together there has to be a conflict. Who can discern the Truth from a lie? Yahwah, the God of Truth. The Creator of Heaven and Earth declares in the book of Malachi 3rd Chapter, verse 17-18. The passage reads:

And they shall be mine, saith the Lord of hosts, in that day when I make up my jewels; and I will spare them, as a man spareth his own son that serveth him.

Then shall ye return, and discern between the righteous and the wicked, between him that serveth God and him that serveth him not.

The Prophets have spoken of the vision of our present era, in days of old. To fulfill their words and his own Will has been the pursuit of the Almighty Creator throughout the ages. Because of man's sin, the light of Truth has been replaced with darkness or confusion in this era. Truth will prevail and Good will triumph, over evil in the end.

Isaiah 10:20-23 speaks specifically of Israel God's chosen. It shows that many Israelites have not escaped Christian indoctrination. The teaching's of Christianity makes spurious claims that God was born of a woman, God died for the sins of man, and that the laws given to Moses have been done-away with. This falsehood was taught to Hebrew Israelites by their Christian slave captors who smote us not long ago.

And it shall come to pass in that day, that the remnant of Israel, and such as are escaped of the house of Jacob, shall no more again stay upon him that smote them; but shall stay upon the Lord, the Holy One of Israel, in truth.

The remnant shall return, even the remnant of Jacob, unto the mighty God.

For though thy people Israel be as the sand of the sea, yet a remnant of them shall return: the consumption decreed shall overflow with righteousness.

For the Lord God of hosts shall make a consumption, even determined, in the midst of all the land.

Few have understood that the Old Testament or Holy Scriptures once existed without a New Testament. The first five books of the Bible tell us that due to sin man has been destined to die. The Holy Scriptures teaches us that the spirit of man does live after death. Elijah and Daniel are spoken of in a context, which indicates their spirits will return in future generations and exist among those living. Reincarnation in this sense is verified in the scriptures. Our ancestors the ancient Israelites understood this.

To find or return to the Laws of GOD is to be symbolically born again. The Eternal One (Spirit) who is from everlasting to everlasting cannot and will never die. Psalm 121:4 states: "The Lord He slumbereth not nor sleepeth". Obviously, a Being who does not sleep nor take a nap, is not a man. The Almighty does not become drowsey or sleepy. The Creator is the Everlasting King of the Universe. He has never abdicated his Throne. There has never been in existence an original Hebrew people, language or culture anywhere in Europe.

The real question is man GOD? Or a god? GOD properly interpreted means Power. Man in a sort of way is a Power. However, the power which man possesses is a limited power. Man is not all-powerful. Furthermore, is man the Creator of the universe, by all reason, who is all powerful? Again, is the CREATOR a man who is limited in every sense? Of course not, or why use attributes such as The ALMIGHTY, The MOST HIGH , the ETERNAL, ALL POWERFUL, OMNIPOTENT, OMNIPRESENT, OMNISCIENT to describe GOD? These are powers and attributes which could <u>not</u> possibly belong to a man.

> *I have said, Ye [are] gods; and all of you [are] children of the most High.*
>
> *But ye shall die like men, and fall like one of the princes*
>
> ***Psalms 82:6-7***

Nothing is clearer than how the Holy Scriptures expresses it's facts on the matter. Consider each of these emphatic statements which consistently state GOD is not a man. This is also a fact upheld throughout the Holy Scriptures. In Genesis 1:1-2, we are told the CREATOR of the universe is a spirit. In Genesis 1:26-27, we are also told He created man.

In Genesis 2:7-8, Again we are told that the CREATOR breathed His spirit into man and he became a living soul as mentioned in Chapter Two of this book. Genesis 2:16-23, says that woman was taken and made from man. Numbers 23:19, 1st Samuel 15:28-31, Hosea 11:7-9, reiterates that YAH is not a man.

If this is indeed the case then the physical appearance of Europeans can in no way be connected to the people of ancient Israel as a biological descendant. Once again, the manner of how Jesus Christ was supposedly born, makes it virtually impossible to have a biological geneology. To be born of the Holy Spirit through an Immaculate Conception, is impossible. Viewed in this light, the increasing debate as to his ethnicity - of African or European extraction, is moot, if the New Testament record is to be believed.

The New Testament is the narrative upon which his life is based. Outside of its doctrine and writings historians and scholars, have been hard pressed to establish factual evidence or traces of his life.

In the book (Ezra Chapter 10:1-4) there is also evidence which shows how the Prophets of Yah viewed the importance of maintaining a pure genealogy within the Israelite Priesthood and nation.

> *Now when Ezra had prayed, and when he had confessed, weeping and casting himself down before the house of God, there assembled unto him out of Israel a very great congregation of men and women and children: for the people wept very sore.*
>
> *And Shechaniah the son of Jehiel, one of the sons of Elam, answered and said unto Ezra, We have trespassed against our God, and have taken strange wives of the people of the land: yet now there is hope in Israel concerning this thing.*
>
> *Now therefore let us make a covenant with our God to put away all the wives, and such as are born of them, according to the counsel of my lord, and of those that tremble at the commandment of our God;*

> *and let it be done according to the law.*
>
> *Arise; for this matter belongeth unto thee: we also will be with thee: be of good courage, and do it.*
>
> ***Ezra 10:1-4***

This issue was so important that men who had taken foreign wives and children put them away. It is clear throughout the Old Testament that Israelites as a whole were not to pollute their seed through mixed marriages. To do so, would defeat the Divine plan and Promise made to Abraham by Yahwah.

It is certainly evident in the Holy Scriptures that the Almighty himself made some exceptions to this rule. However, in each individual case there were special circumstances which brought it about. Joseph for example, was sold into Egypt where he married the wife of an Egyptian Priest " *And Pharaoh called Joseph's name Zaphnath-paaneah; and he gave him to wife Asenath the daughter of Poti-pherah priest of On.* And Joseph went out over all the land of Egypt. (Genesis. Chap. 41:45). Moses also married Jethro's daughter Zipporah, " *And Moses was content to dwell with the man: and he gave Moses Zipporah his daughter.* "(Exodus Chap. 2:21) when he fled from Pharaoh to save his life and lived forty years in Midian.

> Boaz married Ruth *"So Boaz took Ruth, and she was his wife: and when he went in unto her, the Lord gave her conception, and she bore a son.*
>
> *And the women said unto Naomi, Blessed be the Lord, which hath not left thee this day without a kinsman, that his name may be famous in Israel.*
>
> *And he shall be unto thee a restorer of thy life, and a nourisher of thine old age: for thy daughter-in-law, which loveth thee, which is better to thee than seven sons, hath born him.*
>
> *And Naomi took the child, and laid it in her bosom, and became nurse unto it.*

And the women her neighbors gave it a name, saying, There is a son born to Naomi; and they called his name Obed: he is the father of Jesse, the father of David.

Now these are the generations of Pharez: Pharez begot Hezron,

And Hezron begot Ram, and Ram begot Amminadab,

And Amminadab begot Nahshon, and Nahshon begot Salmon,

And Salmon begot Boaz, and Boaz begot Obed,

And Obed begot Jesse, and Jesse begot David.

Ruth 4:13-22

"Now Sarai Abram's wife bore him no children: and she had an handmaid, an Egyptian, whose name was Hagar.

And Sarai said unto Abram, Behold now, the Lord hath restrained me from bearing: I pray thee, go in unto my maid; it may be that I may obtain children by her. And Abram hearkened to the voice of Sarai.

And Sarai Abram's wife took Hagar her maid the Egyptian, after Abram had dwelt ten years in the land of Canaan, and gave her to her husband Abram to be his wife.

Genesis 16:1-3

We read about accounts whereby foreigners were grafted into the genealogy of Israel because of Divine Will. However, as a whole, Israel was forbidden to do so. The Creator sets the rules. He has the right to make exceptions.

The primary reason why foreign marriages were prohibited is explained clearly in Deuteronomy 7:1-4:

> *"When the Lord thy God shall bring thee into the land whither thou goest to possess it, and hath cast out many nations before thee, the Hittites, and the Girgashites, and the Amorites, and the Canaanites, and the Perizzites, and the Hivites, and the Jebusites, seven nations greater and mightier than thou;*
>
> *And when the Lord thy God shall deliver them before thee; thou shalt smite them, and utterly destroy them; thou shalt make no covenant with them, nor show mercy unto them:*
>
> *Neither shalt thou make marriages with them; thy daughter thou shalt not give unto his son, nor his daughter shalt thou take unto thy son.*
>
> ***For they will turn away thy son from following me, that they may serve other gods: so will the anger of the Lord be kindled against you, and destroy thee suddenly.***
>
> ***Deuteronomy** 7: **1-4***

Genealogy is perhaps the area least studied and understood by Bible readers. Most people have probably never noticed the changes and distortions of the Old Testament genealogies recorded in Matthew and Luke. It has been said that the genealogy recorded in Matthew 1:1-23 represents the genealogy traced through Mary to Jesus, and the genealogy recorded in Luke 3:23 represents Joseph's genealogy to Jesus. The genealogy of Israel was always a patriarchal line, meaning it was always passed down through the fathers or male ancestral line and not the mother or female. More importantly, it could only happen by means of a physical biological "sexual" act. The reproduction of every human being created is based on laws and principles of the Creator who made all creatures to reproduce after their own kind.

> *"And God said, Let the earth bring forth the living creature after his kind, cattle, and creeping thing, and beast of the earth after his kind: and it was so.*

And God made the beast of the earth after his kind, and cattle after their kind, and every thing that creepeth upon the earth after his kind: and God saw that it was good.

And God said, Let us make man in our image, after our likeness: and let them have dominion over the fish of the sea, and over the fowl of the air, and over the cattle, and over all the earth, and over every creeping thing that creepeth upon the earth.

So God created man in his own image, in the image of God created he him; male and female created he them.

And God blessed them, and God said unto them, Be fruitful, and multiply, and replenish the earth, and subdue it: and have dominion over the fish of the sea, and over the fowl of the air, and over every living thing that moveth upon the earth.

Genesis 1:24-28

An apple tree reproduces apples; a banana tree reproduces bananas; everything in the creation reproduces after its own kind... man would be no different. The genealogy recorded in the book of Matthews (1:1-6) adheres to this principle entirely.

The book of the generation of Jesus Christ, the son of David, the son of Abraham.

Abraham begat Isaac; and Isaac begat Jacob; and Jacob begat Judas and his brethren;

And Judas begat Phares and Zara of Tamar; and Phares begat Esrom; and Esrom begat Aram;

And Aram begat Aminadab; and Aminadab begat Naasson; and Naasson begat Salmon;

And Salmon begat Boaz of Rahab; and Boaz begat

Obed of Ruth; and Obed begat Jesse;

And Jesse begat David the king; and David the king begat Solomon of her that had been the wife of Uriah.

There is no concrete evidence to prove the existence of such an individual in the history of Israel. It is a case of which came first, the myth or the name. Did the need for a savior create the myth, or did an old Egyptian myth become a new myth in the creation of a Christian deity named, Jesus?

The genealogy given is without a doubt questionable. It is an intermingling of a biological genealogy with a supposed spritual being. This contradicts both Old and new Testament writings. In the Old Testament Genesis 1:24 states: *And God said, Let the earth bring forth the living creature after his kind, cattle, and creeping thing, and beast of the earth after his kind: and it was so.* This is a fundamental law or principle of Yah found in nature and creation. The New Testament also teaches: *" that which is born of the flesh is flesh; and that which is born of the Spirit is spirit." John 3:6*. This means that "spirit cannot reproduce flesh nor can flesh reproduce spirit".

The usual response to this reasoning is that "nothing is impossible for GOD." However, it is impossible for GOD to lie". In Hebrews 6:18 Paul states: *That by two immutable things, in which it was impossible for God to lie, we might have a strong consolation, who have fled for refuge to lay hold upon the hope set before us.*

It has also been argued that GOD, the Creator who is Spirit brought Adam and Eve into existence, who were flesh. Adam was not reproduced by GOD. Adam was made from the ground. The Creator breathed his spirit into the nostrils of Adam and he became a living being. This did not occur through sexual cohabitation with a female. Eve on the other hand, was taken from Adam.

The doctrine which states Jesus, died for our sins must be scrutinized very carefully. Whose sins did he die for? Is it everyone's sin? How could it possibly be? Did he die for them before we committed them? Are we responsible for our sins or is Jesus responsible? Why then have many people been punished for their sins if Jesus died for them? Many people have declared that they can sin because they have been forgiven already, Jesus died for them.

Deuteronomy 22:22, *If a man be found lying with a woman married to a husband, then they shall both of them die, both the man that lay with the woman, and the woman: so shalt thou put away evil from Israel,* is a stern condemnation of this falsely stated act of GOD "If a man be found lying with a woman married to a husband, then shall both of them die, the man that lay with woman and the woman; so shalt thou put away the evil from Israel. Verse 23-24: *If a damsel that is a virgin be betrothed unto a husband, and a man find her in the city, and lie with her; Then ye shall bring them both out unto the gate of that city, and ye shall stone them with stones that they die; the damsel, because she cried not, being in the city; and the man, because he hath humbled his neighbor's wife: so thou shalt put away evil from among you.* "

The just and proper action by Joseph in accordance with the Law was to denounce Mary as an adulteress and demand that both she and the adulterer be stoned to death. Their public example would discourage further violation of the Law and eradicate the evil from the midst of the society. In total contradiction and blasphemy against the Creator, the Greek writings glorify Joseph's actions and perpetrate a blatant lie.

But while he thought on these things, behold the angel of the Lord appeared unto him in a dream, saying, Joseph thou son of David, fear not to take unto thee Mary thy wife, for that which is conceived in her is of the Holy Spirit."

Matthew 20:1

Many Christians insist upon acknowledgement of the Holy Ghost in defiance to Yahwah's Law in which forewarns against consulting a ghost or familiar spirit. Leviticus 19:31 *Turn ye not unto the ghost nor unto familiar spirits; seek them not out, to be defiled by them: I am the Lord your God.* Jesus is erroneously called a son of David, (Matthew 1:1). This actually is Mary's genealogy. This, of course, is in complete disagreement with the manner in which Israelite genealogy is determined which is through the patriarchal or father's genealogy rather than the matriarch or mother's genealogy line. According to Luke 3:23 Jesus is linked with David's genealogy through Joseph.

Teachings as like the one cited below indicate just how Christian doctrine and the New Testament have discouraged the study of genalogy; they are well aware of what an investigation will reveal.

> *As I besought thee to abide still at Ephesus, when I went into Macedonia, that thou mightest charge some that they teach no other doctrine,*
>
> *Neither give heed to fables and endless genealogies, which minister questions, rather than godly edifying which is in faith: so do.*
>
> *Now the end of the commandment is charity out of a pure heart, and of a good conscience, and of faith unfeigned:*
>
> *From which some having swerved have turned aside unto vain jangling;*
>
> *Desiring to be teachers of the law; understanding neither what they say, nor whereof they affirm.*
>
> ***1st Timonthy 1:3-7***

Only until there is mention of the birth of Jesus is this Law or principle changed. Why? Because this is the first major distortion of the truth. The lie and confusion begin at the very beginning of the story recorded in Matthew Chap. 1:18 "*Now the birth of Jesus Christ was on this wise: When as his mother Mary was espoused to Joseph, before they came together, she was found with child of the Holy Ghost.*"

Jesus again, who is he? Ironically Jesus is conveniently force into any precept which has the slightest bit of ambiguity. Sometimes Jesus is GOD, at other times he is the Son of GOD, a Prophet, High Priest, not to mention Father, Son and Holy Ghost. There is no wonder why even Jesus himself wanted to know who they say he is according to Luke 9:18-20, which says:.

> *And it came to pass, as he was alone praying, his disciples were with him: and he asked them, saying, Whom say the people that I am?*
>
> *They answering said, John the Baptist; but some say, Elijah; and others say, that one of the old prophets is risen again.*
>
> *He said unto them, But whom say ye that I am? Peter answering said, The Christ of God.*
>
> ***Luke 9:18-20.***

> *The fathers shall not be put to death for the children, neither shall the children be put to death for the fathers: every man shall be put to death for his own sin.*
>
> ***Deuteronomy 24:16.***

One thing is clear whenever an honest investigation is made into Christian doctrine, there are many concepts recorded in the Holy Scriptures or Old Testament that outright contradict Christian doctrine.

Deuteronomy 24:16 is but another example of this. Christian teachings state that Jesus died for the sins of man. On the contrary, this precept as well as numerous others such as, Leviticus 16:29-34, Ezekiel 18:1-4 and 33:7-12, throughout the Hebrew Scriptures consistently contradict the idea that any human being can be an atonement or sacrifice for the sins of others.

> *And this shall be a statute forever unto you: that in the seventh month, on the tenth day of the month, ye shall afflict your souls, and do no work at all, whether it be one of your own country, or a stranger that sojourneth among you:*

For on that day shall the priest make an atonement for you, to cleanse you, that ye may be clean from all your sins before the Lord.

It shall be a sabbath of rest unto you, and ye shall afflict your souls, by a statute forever.

And the priest, whom he shall anoint, and whom he shall consecrate to minister in the priest's office in his father's stead, shall make the atonement, and shall put on the linen clothes, even the holy garments:

And he shall make an atonement for the holy sanctuary, and he shall make an atonement for the tabernacle of the congregation, and for the altar, and he shall make an atonement for the priests, and for all the people of the congregation.

And this shall be an everlasting statute unto you, to make an atonement for the children of Israel for all their sins once a year. And he did as the Lord commanded Moses.

Leviticus 16:29-34

The word of the Lord came unto me again, saying,

What mean ye, that ye use this proverb concerning the land of Israel, saying, The fathers have eaten sour grapes, and the children's teeth are set on edge?

As I live, saith the Lord God, ye shall not have occasion any more to use this proverb in Israel.

Behold, all souls are mine; as the soul of the father, so also the soul of the son is mine: the soul that sinneth, it shall die.

Ezkekiel 18:1-4

So thou, O son of man, I have set thee a watchman unto the house of Israel; therefore thou shalt hear the word at my mouth, and warn them from me.

When I say unto the wicked, O wicked man, thou shalt surely die; if thou dost not speak to warn the wicked from his way, that wicked man shall die in his iniquity; but his blood will I require at thine hand.

Nevertheless, if thou warn the wicked of his way to turn from it; if he do not turn from his way, he shall die in his iniquity; but thou hast delivered thy soul.

Therefore, O thou son of man, speak unto the house of Israel; Thus ye speak, saying, If our transgressions and our sins be upon us, and we pine away in them, how should we then live?

Say unto them, As I live, saith the Lord God, I have no pleasure in the death of the wicked; but that the wicked turn from his way and live: turn ye, turn ye from your evil ways; for why will ye die, O house of Israel?

Therefore, thou son of man, say unto the children of thy people, The righteousness of the righteous shall not deliver him in the day of his transgression: as for the wickedness of the wicked, he shall not fall thereby in the day that he turneth from his wickedness; neither shall the righteous be able to live for his righteousness in the day that he sinneth.

Ezekiel 33:7-12

Each of the three precepts cited above emphatically stand at odds with Christian teachings on this particular issue that Jesus or anyone else can die for our sins. True justice and reality dictates that each person dies for his/her own sins and is held accountable by our Creator, Yahwah who is a just power.

Just think, a murderer or criminal of any sort telling this to a judge in a court of law in any country. Would the criminal be released or freed on the basis of Jesus dying for his sins? Of course not! Not even if the judge and jury were Christians. Matthew 1:21, states that Jesus would save his people from their sins. The next question is: Who were Jesus' people? According to the New Testament writings the people of Jesus were the Israelites. The doctrine of Christianity says that, Jesus came to save the world. Paul exhorts that Jesus died for the sins of the entire world. This is a contradiction with Matthew's statement. Christianity is a doctrine inundated with confusion and contradictions. But, let's reason together. If Jesus was the son of the Holy spirit, then he has no physical or biological ancestry. He is of a spiritual origin. If his father supposedly is GOD, the Creator who is spirit, Jesus cannot have a link into David's, Joseph's or any other genealogy of man. Everything must reproduce after its own kind.

A lie must be supported by some truth in order to give the appearance of being true. In the case of genealogy, a false genealogy has been merged into the true genealogy of David. This has led many people to believe that the claims made by Christian doctrine are true. However, there is no validity to these claims when the records are examined carefully and understood.

Is it possible that other accounts about the life of Jesus are also fictitious religious beliefs, rather than historical fact?

The genealogy comparison chart of King David's lineage plainly shows just how bogus Christianity teachings are and also discloses the deceptive diabolical manner in which it attempts to merge its lies in with the truth.

COMPARISON OF THE GENEALOGY OF DAVID IN THE OLD AND NEW TESTAMENTS

1st Chronicles 3:1-24

Now these were the sons of David, which were born unto him in Hebon; the first born Amnon, of Ahinoam the Jezreelitess; the second being Daniel, of Abigail the Carmelitess:

The third Absalom the son of Maachah the daughter of Talmai king of Geshur the fourth, Adonijali the son of Haggith;

The fifth, Shephatiah of Abital: the sixth, Ithream by Eglah his wife.

These six were born unto him in Hebron; and there he reigned seven years and six months and in Jerusalem he reigned thirty and three years And these were born unto him in Jerusalem; Shimea, and

Matthew 1:17

The book of the generation of Jesus Christ, the son of david, the son of Abraham. Abraham begat Isaac; and Isaac begat Jacob; and Jacob begat Judas and his brethren; And Judas begat Phares and Zara of Thamar; and Phares begat Esrom. And Esroin begat Aram; And Aram begat Aminadab amd Aininadab begat Naasson and Naasson begat Salmon; And Salmon begat Booz of Rachab and Bo-oz begat Obed of Ruth; and Obed begat Jesse; And Jesse begat David the king: and David the king bei~at Solomon of her that had been the wife of Urias; And Solomon begat Roboam: and Roboam begat Abia: and Abia

St. Luke 3:24-34

And Jesus himself began to be about thirty years of age being(as was supposed) the son of Joseph which was the son of Heli, Which was the son of Mathat, which was the son of Levi, which was the son of Meichi, which was the son of Janna, which was the son of Joseph, Which was the son of Mattathias, which was the son of Amos, which was the son of Naum, which was the son of Esli, which was the son of Nagge Which was the son of Maath, which was the son of Matathias, which ~ras the son of Semei, which was the son of Joseph, which was the son of Juda, Which was the son of Joanna, which was the son of Rhesa,

Shobab, and Nathan, and Solomon, four, of Bathshua the daughter of Ammiel:

Ibhar also, and Elishama, and Eliphelet, And Nogah, and Nepheg, and Japhia, And Elishama, and Elisada, and Eliphelet, nine

These were all the sons of David, beside the sons of the concubines, and Tamar their sister. And Solomon's son was Rehoboam. Abia his son.. Asa his son. Jehoshaphat his son, Joram his son. Ahaziah his son. Joash his son. Amaziah his son. Azariah his son. Jotham his son.

Ahaz hjis son. Hezekiali his son. Manasseh his son

Amon his son. Josiah his son.

And the sons of Josiah his son

And Asa begat Josaphat: and Josaphat begat Joram: and Joram begat Ozias:

And Ozias begat Joatham: and Joatham begat Achaz. and And Ezekias begat Manasses: and Manasses begat Amon; and Amon begat Josias; And Josias begat Jechonias and his brethren. about the time they were carried away to Bablyon:

And after that they were brought to Babylon. Jechonias begat Salathiel: and Salathiel begat Zorobabel:

And Zorobabel begat Abiud: and Abiud begat Eliakim: and Eliakim begat Azor:

And Azor begat Sadoc; and Sadoc begat Achim; and Achim begat Eliud; And Eliud begat

the son of Zorobabel, which was the son of Salatiel;. Which was the son of Neri.

Which was the son of Melchi, which was the son of Addi, which was the son of Cosam, which was the son of Elmodam, which was the son of Er Which was the son of Jose which was the son of Eliezer, which was the son of Jorim, which was the son of Matthat, which was the son of Levi, Which was the son of Simeon, which ws the son of Juda which was the son of Joseph, which was the son of Jonan, which was the son of Eliakim Which was the son of of Melea, which was the son of Menan, which was the son of Mattatha, which was the son of Nathan, which was the son of David, Which was the son of Jesse, which was the son of Obed, which

And the sons of Josiah were, the firstborn Johanan. the second Jehoiakim. the third Zediah. the fourth Shallum

And the sons of Jehoiakim; Jeconioah his son. Zedekiah his son

And the sons of Jeconiali; Assir. Salathiel his son.. Malchiram also, and Pedaiah. and Shenazar.

Achaz begat Ezekias: And the sons of Pedaiah were Zerubbabel. and Shimei and the sons of Zerubbabel: Meshulam, and Hanamah, and Shelomith their sister; and Hashubah, and Ohel, and Berechiah, and Hasadiah, Jushabhesed, five. And the sons of Hananiah:

Pelatiah, and Jeshaiah; the sons of Jeshaiah:

Eleazar; and Eleazar begat Matthan; and Matthan begat Jacob; And Jacob begat Joseph the husband of Mary, of whom was born Jesus, who is called Christ. So all the generations from Abraham to David are fourteen generations; and from David until the carrying away into Babylon are unto Christ Fourteen generations.

was the son of Bo-oz, which was the son of Salmon, which was the son of Naasson Which was the son of Abinadab, which was the son of Aram, which was the son of Esrom.

son of Juda, Which was the son of Jacob, which was the son of Isaac, which was the son Abraham, which was the son of Thara, which was the son of Nachor, Which was the son of Saruch, which was the son of Ragau, which was the son of Phalec, which was the son of Heber, which was the son of Sala, Which was the son of Cainan, which was the son of Arphaxad, which was the son of Sem, which was the son of Noe, which was the son of Lamech, Which was the son of Mathusala, which was the son of Epoch, which was the son of Jared,

Rephaiah; the sons of Rephaiali: Arnan; the sons of Arnan:

Obadiah; the sons of Obadiah: Shecamah. And the sons of Shecaniab: Shemaiah; and the sons of Shemaiah: Hattush, and Igal, and Bariah, and Neariah, and Shaphat, six. And the sons of Neariali: Elioenai and Hizkiah, and Azrikam, three. And the sons of Elioenai: Hodaviah, and Eliashib, and Pelajab, and Akkub, and Johanan, and Delaiah, and Anani, seven..

which was the son of Maleleel, which ws the son of Cainan, Which was the son of Enos, which was the son of Seth, which was the son of Adam, which was the son of God.

CHRISTMAS, EASTER AND THE APPOINTED SEASONS

There are some fundamental facts which are neither, considered nor known by many people about Christianity. Christmas and Easter in particular are prime examples. Neither Christmas nor Easter are mentioned anywhere in the Bible. In fact, both of these Christian religious observances are based on pagan holidays and customs. There is no commandment or edict to observe or celebrate Christmas or Easter. They are not Holy days, they are man-made holidays. All Holy days, which are called appointed seasons, are written about in the book of Leviticus, and established by Yahwah himself. If a Holy Day is not recorded in Leviticus the 23rd Chapter, it is not mandated or approved by Yah.

It is sad to think that millions of parents who work extremely hard to purchase gifts for their children, then turn around and tell their children that Santa Claus brought the gifts for them. These same parents attempt to teach their children to be honest and truthful. But, start early in the child's life as an adult liar, about one of the most sensitive subjects in their lives, the origin of Yah. These parents are also responsible for the perpetuation of this lie, which has proven to be psychologically damaging to children.

Christmas is the day on which Christians celebrate the birth of Jesus Christ. No one knows exactly when Jesus was born and there has been much speculation as to whether it was winter, fall or spring. The most commonly agreed upon date for Jesus' birth is December 25th but some Christians celebrate his birthday on January 6th. Numerous Eastern people believe it would be impossible for the event stated in Luke 2:8 to have taken place during the winter season simply because, sheperds in that region of the world would only appear with their flocks during the fall season which occurs around October, not in December.

> *And there were in the same country shepherds abiding in the field, keeping watch over their flock by night.*

And, lo, the angel of the Lord came upon them, and the glory of the Lord shone round about them: and they were sore afraid.

And the angel said unto them, Fear not: for, behold, I bring you good tidings of great joy, which shall be to all people.

For unto you is born this day in the city of David a Savior, which is Christ the Lord.

And this shall be a sign unto you; Ye shall find the babe wrapped in swaddling clothes, lying in a manger.

Luke 2:8-12

The narrative cited in Luke is used to tell the story of Christmas. However, the word Christmas comes from the early English phrase "Christ's Masse" which means Christ's Mass. In Catholicism, which is the first of all Christian denominations Christ Mass," the "Mass" represents the religious ceremony associated with the celebration of the birth of Christ. The word "Mass" is not the term associated with Christmas ceremonies in other Christian denominations.

The fact that millions of people worldwide begin to prepare for Christmas weeks and even months before the day arrives, seem to help set a mood of joy, happiness and good cheer at Christmas time. Therefore, no consideration is given to the origin of Christian practices by most people. The emotion and revelry associated with Christmas has provided little or no room for historical investigation.

Undoubtedly, there are many Christians who would admit that Christmas has become nothing more than a commercial holiday void of any true religious significance. Throughout the year factories manufacture lights, ornaments, and decorative items for homes and Christmas trees. Thousands of Christmas trees are grown and sold. Millions of greeting cards are designed and manufactured for sale. The United States Postal Service hires extra employees to speed the delivery of millions of cards mailed during December. The purchase of Christmas gifts for relatives and friends increases business to the extent that as much as a quarter of the yearly sales of many stores come at Christmas time.

The sale of Christmas music is also a booming business. This has brought tremendous popularity to the celebration of Christmas. The artificial celebration of peace on earth and the brotherhood of mankind is no doubt an attraction to many Christians, as well as non-Christians. The media has also been very instrumental in the widespread influence and attention paid to Christmas worldwide. Unlike, holiday celebrations of other religions, the Christmas holiday receives more media coverage than any other celebrated holiday in the world.

Christmas is observed in many different ways throughout the world with customs varying from country to country. In many places, Christmas customs are based on indigenous traditions, rather than any early or original Christmas traditions.

In Italy, the people fast, going with little or no food at all, on Christmas Day. In the evening, the family holds a ceremony around the "presepio". This is a miniature scene of Bethlehem with tiny figures of the Holy Family, shepherds and wise men.

Few Christians live in Asian countries. Even where Christianity does exist in Asia, the celebration of Christmas as a religious festival is rare. Asian Christians do tend to sing carols in the same manner as Western Christians but for the most part, they prefer to keep to the various indigenous culture and practices. In the Philippines, the Christmas season lasts 22 days, from December 16th to January 6th.

The Armenians observe their Christmas on January 6th in Roman Catholic, Anglican, Eastern, and other Christian churches. Originally it celebrated both the birth and the baptism of Jesus. Since the 4th century AD it has honored the meeting of the three wise men (magi) with the infant Jesus. In some countries, doorways are marked with the initials of the three wise men to keep evil away.

In Iran, people call Christmas "The Little Feast." For the first 24 days of December, Christians in Iran eat no meat, milk or eggs. On Christmas, they feast. In Syria, Christians believe that the trees bow their heads on the eve of Epiphany in honor of the Christ child.

In most of Africa, Christmas customs and observances were introduced by missionaries and generally follow western practices. Christians of the Eastern Orthodox churches in Egypt celebrated Christmas on January 6th. which is still the practice to this date.

The symbols associated with Christmas in many ways speak of the manner in which Christianity has borrowed ideas from various countries. Over a long period of time the transfiguration of the old or the original idea is changed so greatly that people become skeptical of the old idea which was actually replaced by the new.

The custom of exchanging Christmas gifts is said to have begun in memory of the gifts the wise men brought the Christ child. In some countries, children believe the wise men or the Christ child brings them gifts. In some countries, children believe their gifts come from Saint Nicholas, a Bishop famous for his generosity. However, the most celebrated gift giver is Santa Claus.

Saint Nicholas, who served as the Bishop of Myra, in Asia Minor, during the 4th century AD became famous for his generosity, especially toward children. Gradually he became known as the patron saint of children. His feast day is December 6th and he was believed to bring gifts to children on the eve of that day. Over time, he became accepted as the gift giver at Christmas time. Saint Nicholas acquired different names in different countries.

Santa Claus is a distinctly American symbol of Christmas. He gets his name from the early Dutch settlers in New York who calls Saint Nicholas "Sinterklaas." As it became more American, he took on some of the non-religious characteristics known today. For example, the belief that Santa enters the house through the chimney developed from an Old Norse legend. The Norse believed that the goddess Hertha appeared in the fireplace and brought good luck to the house.

In 1822, Clement C. Moore, an American Minister and poet, first described Santa's fur trimmed suit and his sleigh pulled by reindeer. The description appears in Moore's Famous poem " A Visit from St. Nicholas" called the "Night Before Christmas." In the later 1800's, Thomas Nast an American cartoonist, did a series of drawings that established Santa Claus as the big roly-poly figure of today.

A number of legends are cited as the source of the first Christmas tree. Some mention the English missionary Winfird, later called Bonaface. As he traveled through Northern Germany, he met a group of Druids who were about to sacrifice young Prince Asulf to the God Thor, to whom the oak was sacred. Winfred was able to stop the sacrifice. He told the Druids that the fir tree was to be their new holy tree. He said that its wood provided homes for them and that it was the tree of peace and the tree of Christ.

In the early 1400's and 1500's the Germans were probably the first to use Christmas tree decorations. Another legend has it that Martin Luther the leader of the Protestant Reformation started the custom of decorating Christmas trees. Scandinavians were the first to trim their trees with fishnets and little flags. People of Poland decorate trees with bright paper ornaments and candles.Today Americans use string of colored electric lights.

The Romans exchanged green tree branches for good on the first day of January (Calends). The English took this custom over for Christmas. The burnin of the Yule log began as a custom among ancient Scandinavians, who once a year burned a huge log in honor of their god Thor. Later the Yule log became important in England as well as other countries.

Mistletoe decorates many homes in the United States, Canada and Europe at Christmas time. In Scandinavia, mistletoe was considered the plant of peace. If enemies met under it, they declared a truce for the day. Some believe this is the origin of the present custom of kissing whomever stands beneath a sprig of mistletoe.

The first hymns written especially for Christmas date back to the 4th Century A.D.. They were written in Latin and dealt with theological subjects. In the 13th, 18th and 19th centuries acting out the Nativity and the writing of christmas carols flourished in Europe. Christmas, as we know it is a European creation, which has nothing to do with the Creator of Heaven and earth. The brief historical background presented here shows that people can lose contact with the facts and truth about things as history evolves. This has certainly been the case with Christianity and the various customs associated with it.

> **CHRISTMAS** was a work or school day for many Americans until the mid 1800's. The traditional American Christmas, in fact, is not so very old at all. Gift giving, card sending, tree trimming and other present day customs did not become widely popular until the final decades of the 19th century arriving then as a package of Victorian style and business zeal.
>
> For many years, Thanksgiving actually was far more special than Christmas in New England. In the south, firecrackers were set off on Christmas morning; colored eggs decorated evergreens in Dutch settlements among the Hudson River, and well into the 1800's, Santa Claus was portrayed as quite a small elfish figure sometimes capped off with a feather.
>
> "Technological developments, advances in transportation, printing and mail services probably were responsible for the enormous change and popularization of Christmas day in the Victorian period," according to Shriley Cherkasky, a sociologist responsible for holiday research at the Smithsonian Institution's Division of Performing Arts, in Washington, D.C.
>
> Certainly the publication of Charles Dickens "Christmas Carol," with its themes of charity and good will affected the idea of how people felt Christmas should be observed," she adds.

The Puritans associated Christmas with the Church of England, a painful reminder of their struggle for religious freedom. The December 25 holiday, they strongly felt, was a human invention, a fabrication: Christ's birthday was unknown; therefore the Church should never have ordained the day. The Puritans also didn't care much for the occasion, thinking it too closely linked to the spirited pagan celebration of the winter solstice.

Early in the country's history, the Puritan settlers believed that Christmas should not be observed at all, and in 1659 the celebration was outlawed in Massachusetts by the decree: "Who ever shall be found observing any such day as Christmas and the like, shall pay for each offense five shillings to the country."

But in New York, Pennsylvania and the Southern colonies, Christmas was another matter altogether. The Anglicans, Lutherans, Dutch Reformed and Catholics in these regions celebrated with music, dancing, feast and family gatherings. A French traveler, visiting the home of a Virginian in the 1680's reported: "There was a great deal of carousing. He had sent for three fiddlers, a jester a tightrope dancer, an acrobat who tumbled... they gave us all the entertainment one could wish for."

"Today," Cherkasky notes, "if you're talking about getting back to a more religious holiday, you might remember that Christmas used to be pretty wild." So wild that one early custom called mumming – knocking on doors, ringing bells, rattling cans and shooting off firearms – got completely out of hand in Baltimore late in the 1800's, falling into decline when quieter residents complained.

After years of struggle, the Massachusetts Puritans in 1681 repealed their anti-holiday decree, apparently won over by two reasons: the seasonal joy they could see their neighbors experiencing, and the U.S. Constitution later gave protection to the separation of church and state. The Puritans, according to social historian James II Barnett, were less inclined to oppose the secular celebration when it was no longer a symbol of the political and religious dominance of the Church of England.

But some in the colony still were not reconciled to the decision. Complained one Judge Sewell: "I believe that the body of the people profane it; and blessed be God. No authority yet to compel them to keep it." In 1858 though, Massachusetts joined the growing list of states giving legal recognition to Christmas Day first being Alabama 20 years earlier.

By the mid 1800's, Christmas spirit was on the upswing throughout the country. Dickens' "A Christmas Carol," published in 1843 helped bridge local and regional differences in holiday customs. Its themes of kindness and generosity according to Cherkasky, crossed many cultural and regional boundaries, thereby helping to universalize the Christmas celebration.

In 1867 Dickens gave reading of the tale in the United States, including New York. After one appearance, he wrote, "They took it so tremendously last night that I was stopped every five minutes. One poor young girl burst into a passion of grief about Tiny Tim and had to be taken out."

As it did in other areas of American life, the Industrial Revolution began to influence the way Christmas was observed. Christmas cards, for example, could be produced and mailed inexpensively, gaining wide popularity by 1875. And for better or worse, the first holiday advertising appeared in 1830's.

But it was not until late in the century when the business and pleasure of gift giving began in earnest that elaborate Christmas celebrations became an annual American experience. "Gifts at first were given mainly to children, servants and trades people." Cherkasky notes: "It was a time for evening up accounts. But that was all to change."

"The folk secular aspect of Christmas was taking precedence over its religious one," historian Barnett says. "This was apparent in the increasing importance of Santa Claus." Thomas Nast's drawings in Harper's weekly portrayed Santa for the first time as a jolly, white-bearded character dressed in fur.

The popularity of the Christmas tree grew right along with the change in social customs and technological progress. After Queen Victoria set up a Yuletide tree at Windsor Castle, the style was set, reaching the White House in 1855 during Franklin Pierce's presidency.

Thomas Edison's lab came up with a string of tree lights in 1882, three years after the incandescent light break through, and immediate this novel idea became the rage among the wealthy Christmas tree parties to show off the expensive lighted trees were major social events.

Today, of course, the Christmas season is the sum of many traditions.

Daily News, Sunday, December 23, 1979

Easter is a Christian festival that celebrates the resurrection of Jesus Christ. It is viewed by many Christians as the most important day of the Christian religion. The birth of Jesus is celebrated on December 25th the last month in the year. His resurrection is celebrated before his birth. Easter is usually celerated in March or April. Now if Jesus were God, as some Christians claim, how could he die - particularly when the scriptures are explicitly clear that the Creator of heaven and earth is everlasting? Moses declares in the 90th Psalm "From Everlasting to Everlasting thou art God." Indeed, the eternity of God is maintained in the Old Testament.

The name Easter is said to have derived from Istar or Astarte, a Babylonian deity. Istar or Astarte represented the moon, which was known to them as the Queen Mother of Heaven. The custom of wearing new clothing and dressing up for the Queen Mother of Heaven also began in Mesopotamia among the Babylonians. The word Easter appears no where in the Bible. Neither are the practices associated with it written anywhere in the Bible. However, the story of Easter has been based on the Gospels written in the New Testament, which tell that the body of Jesus disappeared from the tomb on the third day after his crucifixion.

Some of the symbols associated with Easter have actually been taken from other cultures. Traditions known to us today are quite removed from the original practices and meanings.

One of symbols of Easter is the cross, a modification of one of the ancient Roman methods of punishing criminals. In ancient Rome, criminals were often crucified by nailing them to a tree or post with the feet together and the arms spread. Interestingly enough, some Christian writings even claim that this was the actual fashion that Jesus was killed. Nevertheless, Christians have appropriated the symbol of the cross and tied it to the crucifixion of Jesus Christ. It developed into a special meaning to Christians as a symbol of Christ's alleged victory over death. The cross often appears as an Easter symbol in many forms. For instance, people in many parts of the world eat special pasteries called **"hot cross buns"** during the Easter season. Each pastry has a cross filled with a custard.

Easter decorations and paintings often include the figure of a lamb as a symbol of Jesus. Lamb is one of the traditional Easter foods and cookies and cakes shaped like lambs decorate many tables at Easter time. The symbol of the lamb comes from the Israelite Passover or Pesach. The Israelites were commanded to sacrifice a Lamb or Goat for the Passover feast held on 14th day of Aviv, the first month on the Hebrew or lunar calendar, at Dusk in the Temple in Jerusalem.

And the Lord spoke unto Moses and Aaron in the land of Egypt, saying,

This month shall be unto you the beginning of months: it shall be the first month of the year to you.

Speak ye unto all the congregation of Israel, saying, In the tenth day of this month they shall take to them every man a lamb, according to the house of their fathers, a lamb for a house:

And if the household be too little for the lamb, let him and his neighbor next unto his house take it according to the number of the souls; every man according to his eating shall make your count for the lamb.

Your lamb shall be without blemish, a male of the first year: ye shall take it out from the sheep, or from the goats:

And ye shall keep it up until the fourteenth day of the same month: and the whole assembly of the congregation of Israel shall kill it in the evening.

And they shall take of the blood, and strike it on the two side posts and on the upper door post of the houses, wherein they shall eat it.

And thus shall ye eat it; with your loins girded, your shoes on your feet, and your staff in your hand; and ye shall eat it in haste: it is the Lord's passover.

Exodus12:1-7, 11

Observe the month of Abib, and keep the passover unto the Lord thy God: for in the month of Abib the Lord thy God brought thee forth out of Egypt by night.

Thou shalt therefore sacrifice the passover unto the

> *Lord thy God, of the flock and the herd, in the place which the Lord shall choose to place his name there.*

Early Christians interpreted the sacrifice of the Passover Lamb as a forecast of Christ's sacrifice or crucifixion on the cross. They spoke of Jesus as "The Lamb of GOD", which taketh away the sins of the world." The fact of matter is that the sins of the world have steadily increased reaching what can be called an all time high.

> *The next day John seeth Jesus coming unto him, and saith, Behold the Lamb of God, which taketh away the sin of the world.*
>
> ***John 1:29***

Roman Catholics light candles from a new fire on Easter Eve, they call it the Paschal Candle or Easter candle. They use this candle to relight all the candles from the great paschal candle and carry them home where they can be used on special occasion. In many parts of Northern and Central Europe, people burn bonfires on the hilltops. They also gather around the bonfires and sing Easter hymns.

The search for Easter eggs is another practice that has no Biblical origin In fact, the egg was an ancient fertility symbol to a number of pagan religions - the very ones that the Creator admonished His people from following. The Christians of Ancient Egypt and Persia often dyed eggs in spring colors and gave them to their friends as gifts. The Persians believed that the earth had hatched from a giant egg. Many children believe that an Easter bunny brings their Easter eggs. This belief probably comes from Germany where legends say that a poor woman dyed some eggs during a famine, and hid them in a nest as an Easter gift for her children. Just as the children discovered the nest, a large rabbit leaped away.The story spread that the rabbit had brought the Easter eggs. Naturally, with so many different denominations of Christianity there has never been a uniform manner for the observance of Easter. Most Christians are totally unaware of how other countries and denominations observe or celebrate Easter. Moreover, there are vast differences in Christmas beliefs and doctrine, how the various groups practice Christianity. Nowadays, as one travels throughout the world, it is common to come across hundreds of Christian groups which have split and developed doctrines far from mainstream Christianity.

In gaining the correct understanding of the appointed seasons, we must understand the vast differences in the manner in which time was marked according to the ancient Hebrew calender, versus the Gregorian calendar which holds sway over much of the modern world.

The Hebrew calendar consists of twelve months. Their names are Aviv, Siw, Siwan, Tammuz, Av, Elul, Etanim, Bul, Kislev, Tevet, Shavat and Adar. Aviv is the first month of the year, which begins spring. All appointed seasons and Holydays are determined in accordance with the lunar cycle. In addition, the various different "cycles of planting and harvesting fall within a time frame that is in accordance with the solar cycles. The Holy days found in the Old Testament have been in existence far longer than those established by Christianity and all other European religions that have sprung from it..

On the contrary, the Gregorian European calendar, named after Pope Gregory (540-604 AD), came into existence through several modifications of previous Roman calendars. The early Roman calendar consisted of ten months; January and February were added to the months of the year in order to collect additional taxes in the year. The Gregorian months are January, February, March, April, May, June, July, August, September, October, November, December.

As we have seen, the holidays within the Gregorian calendar have adopted and absorbed their customs and traditions from among many peoples but have no biblical foundation.

HOLY DAY AND HOLIDAY COMPARISION

Hebrew Holy Days ***Leviticus 23***	**Christian Holidays** ***Mentioned no where in the Bible***
Sabbath - 7th Day	Sabbath - 1st Day
Passover	New Years Day
Feast of Unleavened Bread	Lent
Feast of Weeks	Easter
Day of the Blowing of the Horn	Pentecost
Day of Atonement	Christmas
Feast of Booths	Halloween - All Saints Day
Eight-Day Solemn Assembly	St. Valentine
	St. Patrick's Day

Non-Holy Day Observances
Exodus 12:1
New Year's Day 1st of Aviv

Isaiah 66:23
New Moon

WEEKDAY COMPARISION

The Gregorian weekday names represent stars, planets and Greek gods which were worshiped at the time.

Hebrew Weekday Names	**Gregorian Weekday Names**
Yom Achad - Day 1	Sunday - Sun god
Yom Shenee - Day 2	Monday - Moon god
Yom Sh'leshe - Day 3	Tuesday - Mars god
Yom Re-vee-ee - Day 4	Wednesday- Odin/Woden the Norse god
Yom Kameeshee - Day 5	Thursday - Thor god
Yom She'shee - Day 6	Friday - Friggs, Scandinavian god
Yom She've'ee - Day 7 *(Shabbat)*	Saturday - Planet Saturn god

As mentioned earlier in the text Israelites were forbidden to mention the names of other gods. *Exodus 23:13* Also note that the name Tamuz is the name of a Babylonian god and therefore Israelites generally do not use the name but subsitute it for the number of the month.

THE LAW

Ye shall not add unto the word which I command you, neither shall ye diminish ought from it, that ye may keep the commandments of the LORD your God which I command you.

Deuteronomy 4:2

The word law in the Holy scriptures is derived from the Hebrew word Torah (תורה) which means instructions and teachings known as commandments, statues and judgments. Is man still under the Law, or is he released by Grace? This debate, as much as anything, epitomizes one of the major differences between Old Testament and New Testament teachings. For Christians, the Law, particularly as misinterpreted over the centuries, has no place in society. It is harsh, cruel, archaic... and in the words of Paul, "condemning." Christians, the logic goes, have been freed from the condemnation and imperfection of the Law (as if Yah could author anything flawed) and are somehow rendered unaccountable, by Grace. Yet even the most cursory examination of the Laws of the Creation, deemed "science" show that for every action, there is a relative response. Jump off a high building and you'll probably die. Stand in front of a moving car, and chances are, it will kill you, if not seriously injure you. Now if by some quirk of fate the fall or the speeding car don't kill you, folks might rightly attribute that to a miracle (which in itself is an assertion that something other than what was supposed to occur, took place). But you certainly won't hear their survival attributed to Grace. If anything you'll hear someone rightly say "they had no business jumping off that roof, or standing in front of that speeding car." Grace will not save you from any of these logical conclusions. So is Yah's Law designed to save man from the logical, natural conclusions of wrong actions.

With all humility I appeal to our sincere reasoning and ask "How can we on earth believe our creator has abandon his divine plan for human existence." No orderly man-made society is built upon Grace. Mankind from the highest to the lowest espouses the need for Laws, in order for society to flourish. You break societies laws, and you receive the relative result. And, even in man-made societies, ignorance of the Law is no excuse. Nowhere in the civilized world can a person commit a crime, and be acquitted, merely on a defense that they were unaware it was a crime. Likewise, when it comes to the Laws of the Creator, a person is guilty of sin, whether it is known or unknown to him. In other words, jump off a building high enough to kill you, and you'll die, regardless of whether or not you knew it would kill you. When we look at our poisoned bodies from poor diets, the poisoned societies from poor or weak rules (and an abscence of respect for them), we can see that now, more than evermore, the Law that "was done away with," is sorely needed.

To claim that the Laws of Yah were done away with because of Israel's inability to obey or keep them or because of a new dispensation such as Jesus' birth and death for the sins of Israel and all mankind is absurd. Moreover, it is a gross distortion of the facts and the truth. Whenever a people are taken captive to foreign lands their Constitution ceases. It does not mean that their Laws are destroyed, abolished or done away with. It is strictly due to the circumstances created by their loss of independence as a free people. The Law of Yah is the constitution of the Nation of Israel, and ultimately would be that of the whole of the Creation. The Prophets brought the Laws, that Yah's order would reign supreme, that there would be some clear instructions of what man was supposed to do in order to maintain his holiness, health, societal order and ultimately, his sanctification, in the eyes of the Creator Yahwah.

The true worship of the true and living power (God) is a matter of truth or consequences. There is no other savior. There is no one else who can deliver anyone out of his hand or from his judgment. In Hebraic thought, death in spiritual sense is understood as living without knowledge of Yahwah (God) and his laws. These Laws are eternal and perfect because they come directly from Yah, and are not mixed with any opinions or commentary by man. In fact, nowhere in the entire Old Testament is there a single instance where an Inspired Prophet of God has given his opinion. The law states that any Prophet who speaks contrary to the Laws of Yah is not to be regarded as a true Prophet sent by

Him. Consistent with this view is the point that the people of Israel were not to hearken to a Prophet who spoke in the name of other gods. The Law also states that only an Israelite is to be accepted as a Prophet sent to them. Even an Israelite Prophet is guilty if he attempts to change the Law. Christianity in the eyes of some scholars should be named Paulism because Christian teachings are actually primarily based on the belief and opinions of Paul, as expressed in his epistles or letters. Few of the purported sayings expressed by Jesus Christ are maintained within Christianity. He himself made his position on the Law clear, as recorded in the Gospels. So even this mythical savior, they purport to believe, is at most times in accordance with the Old Testament Canon. Yet, the epistles, the personal writings of Paul are what seem to hold sway over the majority of Christianity The opinions or personal viewpoints of Paul often contradict what Jesus has allegedly said in the Greek writings and certainly contradict the Law and word of Yahwah in the Holy Scriptures which is the authority.

What will follow in the rest of this chapter, is a brief examination of some of the Creator's Laws, contained in the Old Testament, compared to the contradictions of the New Testament. Because man on earth has violated the Creator's laws and broken the everlasting covenant, many curses exist among us. HIV, AIDS, hepatitis herpes and gonorrhea exist because of widespread promiscuity. Teenage pregnancies have caused enormous social consequences as well. Rape, sexual abuse of our children and homosexuality are attributed to not acknowledging the laws of Yahwah. Adult violence, Teenage violence, robbery, theft, in high places and low places, coupled with inequality and double standards of law has brought our prisons to an overwhelming capacity. These sins and more are all examples of how we are violating the laws written in the Bible.

> *But we know that the law is good, if a man use it lawfully;*
>
> *Knowing this, that the law is not made for a righteous man, but for the lawless and disobedient, for the ungodly and for sinners, for unholy and profane, for murderers of fathers and murderers of mothers, for manslayers,*

For whoremongers, for them that defile themselves with mankind, for menstealers, for liars, for perjured persons, and if there be any other thing that is contrary to sound doctrine;

According to the glorious gospel of the blessed God, which was committed to my trust.

1st Timothy 1:8-11

Here is another example of contradiction and trickery combined in an attempt to nullify the law. The Law states; "nothing should be added to the it nor anything diminished from it." In the book of John, Jesus asks for which one of the miracles have you rejected me? The reply by his accusers is, "For none of the good works do we reject thee, but because thou being a man and makest thyself God, do we reject." It is inferred by the New Testament account that Jesus spoke about forgiving sins, which is an exclusive power of God. Jesus also spoke contrary to Law in the New Testament on the issue of Sabbath observance. This too is a violation. No man has the power to do so. Personal opinions can never supercede the Law or word of God. The Law States that the Sabbath is the Day of Rest. No work is permitted on that day.

And the Lord spoke unto Moses, saying, Speak thou also unto the children of Israel, saying, Verily my sabbaths ye shall keep: for it is a sign between me and you throughout your generations; that ye may know that I am the Lord that doth sanctify you.

Ye shall keep the sabbath therefore; for it is holy unto you: every one that defileth it shall surely be put to death: for whosoever doeth any work therein, that soul shall be cut off from among his people.

Six days may work be done; but in the seventh is the sabbath of rest, holy to the LORD: whosoever doeth any work in the sabbath day, he shall surely be put to death.

Wherefore the children of Israel shall keep the sab-

bath, to observe the sabbath throughout their generations, for a perpetual covenant.

It is a sign between me and the children of Israel for ever: for in six days the LORD made heaven and earth, and on the seventh day he rested, and was refreshed.

Exodus 31:12-17

On the contrary Jesus says in Luke 6:1-5:

And it came to pass on the second sabbath after the first, that he went through the corn fields; and his disciples plucked the ears of corn, and did eat, rubbing them in their hands.

And certain of the Pharisees said unto them, Why do ye that which is not lawful to do on the sabbath days

And Jesus answering them said, Have ye not read so much as this, what David did, when himself was hungry, and they which were with him;

How he went into the house of God, and did take and eat the shewbread, and gave also to them that were with him; which it is not lawful to eat but for the priests alone?

And he said unto them, That the Son of man is Lord also of the sabbath.

The evidence surrounding the New Testament writings indicate that they were produced approximately four decades to over a century after the death of the Christian savior. Why? Is it an accurate account of the facts? There are numerous unanswerable questions and an untold number of undeniable paradoxical ideas which are beyond any logical reasoning. There is nothing written anywhere within the Old Testament which could in any wise equal or compare with the New Testament's self condemnation. The statement "God is not the author of confusion" is epitomized in the New Testament because the writings are founded upon utter confusion and unsubstantiated truths.

For God is not the author of confusion, but of peace, as in all churches of the saints.

I Corinthians 14:33

And on the seventh day God ended his work which he had made; and he rested on the seventh day from all his work which he had made.

And God blessed the seventh day, and sanctified it: because that in it he had rested from all his work which God created and made.

Genesis 2:2-3

And the LORD spake unto Moses, saying,

Speak unto the children of Israel, and say unto them, Concerning the feasts of the LORD, which ye shall proclaim to be holy convocations, even these are my feasts.

Six days shall work be done: but the seventh day is the sabbath of rest, an holy convocation; ye shall do no work therein: it is the sabbath of the LORD in all your dwellings.

Leviticus 23:1-3

Behold, the days come, saith the Lord, that I will make a new covenant with the house of Israel, and with the house of Judah:

Not according to the covenant that I made with their fathers in the day that I took them by the hand to bring them out of the land of Egypt; which my covenant they broke, although I was a husband unto them, saith YAHWAH:

But this shall be the covenant that I will make with the house of Israel; After those days, saith YAHWAH,

I will put my law in their inward parts, and write it in their hearts; and will be their God, and they shall be my people.

And they shall teach no more every man his neighbor, and every man his brother, saying, Know YAHWAH: for they shall all know me, from the least of them unto the greatest of them, saith YAHWAH: for I will forgive their iniquity, and I will remember their sin no more.

Thus saith the LORD, which giveth the sun for a light by day, and the ordinances of the moon and of the stars for a light by night, which divideth the sea when the waves thereof roar; The LORD of hosts is his name:

If those ordinances depart from before me, saith the LORD, then the seed of Israel also shall cease from being a nation before me for ever.

Thus saith the LORD; If heaven above can be measured, and the foundations of the earth searched out beneath, I will also cast off all the seed of Israel for all that they have done, saith the LORD.

Jeremiah 31:31-37

In this prophecy Jeremiah foretells of the time when YAH will restore His covenant with a new sense of influence upon the regulated thoughts in the minds of His people Israel. The inner spirits of the Israelites returning to the covenant Law will be blessed with the knowledge of the Law. By literally having YAHWAH put the Law in the mind, spirit and soul of Israel. Therefore as commandment keepers, Israel, will become a righteous people and nation.

This is strictly, a prophecy directed, solely to the renewed relationship, of the returning exiled nation of Israelites, who will become, obedient to the very Laws, they once rejected. As a result of their obedience YAHWAH will become their GOD once again and accept them as His people. Unlike their past experiences, in the future, all Israel will know GOD, YAHWAH from the greatest person a king, to the least person, common man. Christians have taken the phrase "new covenant" and completely distorted the contents of these ideas with a grossly modified explanation applied in their doctrine, which states that the Law has been done away with as of the death of Jesus Christ.

"B'reet" ברית "covenant" in Hebrew is the Law. Israel agreed to do the Law and YAHWAH agreed He would be their POWER, if they would keep His Laws. Here, the new covenant means a new manner in which Israel would know YAH and obey His Laws. The exact same Laws would be placed within them in the future. This is a major contradiction to Christian teachings. Furthermore, the forgiveness of their sins will be an act of Yahwah based upon their acceptance and keeping of the laws rather than the Christian version of salvation with forgiveness through the belief of Jesus Christ.

How could Jesus forgive them, when it was YAH, ALMIGHTY who scattered and punished them for their sins against Him, not Jesus. Therefore, it is ridiculous to think that anyone else could forgive their sins. This prophecy clearly applies strictly to YAHWAH and His restoration of His people, Israel, and it has nothing to do with Jesus or Christianity. Jesus was not a savior. The Holy Scriptures clearly states that Yahwah will turn the captivity of His chosen people Israel and they will return, obey, and keep His Laws, as they were instructed in days of old. Malachi 4:2-6 states.

> *But unto you that fear my name shall the Sun of righteousness arise with healing in his wings; and ye shall go forth, and grow up as calves of the stall.*
>
> *And ye shall tread down the wicked; for they shall be ashes under the soles of your feet in the day that I shall do this, saith the Lord of hosts.*
>
> *Remember ye the law of Moses my servant, which I commanded unto him in Horeb for all Israel, with the statutes and judgments.*

It has also been falsely taught in Christian doctrine that the ceremonial laws of offerings were done away with because of the death of Jesus. The people of Israel, priests in particular, are commanded by law to perform offerings at appointed times. For example, daily offerings, Sabbath offerings, New Moon and Holy Day offerings. (Numbers 28 and 29) In addition, the priests were commaded to make burnt offerings, guilt offerings, sin offerings, meal offerings, drink offerings, peace offerings, free will offerings and thanksgiving offerings at the appropriate times. Many Christian ministers assert the point of view that God no longer desires offerings because Jesus was the sacrificial lamb, which abolished sin. They also erroneously purport that the law has been replaced by grace. As a result, people feel they are unaccoutable for their wrong doings, sins and violations of the Creator's laws. Therefore, Christian doctrine teaches that offerings are strictly a thing of the past. Ezekiel 44:15-31; is a vision concerning the end of days when Israel would have returned to Jerusalem and Israel the Holy Land. The passage reads:

> *But the priests the Levites, the sons of Zadok, that kept the charge of my sanctuary when the children of Israel went astray from me, they shall come near to me to minister unto me, and they shall stand before me to offer unto me the fat and the blood, saith the Lord God:*
>
> *They shall enter into my sanctuary, and they shall come near to my table, to minister unto me, and they shall keep my charge.*
>
> *And it shall come to pass, that when they enter in at the gates of the inner court, they shall be clothed with linen garments; and no wool shall come upon them, while they minister in the gates of the inner court, and within.*
>
> *They shall have linen bonnets upon their heads, and shall have linen breeches upon their loins; they shall not gird themselves with any thing that causeth sweat.*

CIVIL AND MORAL LAWS

Today we live in a world full of debauchery, void of moral conduct, civil rights and justice. It is sad to think that some people believe or purport the theory that righteousness, morality, virtue and integrity are no longer necessary. On the contrary, the Holy Scriptures indicate that principles set down by our Everlasting Father are eternal Laws.

When we compare these essential rules, which have been given by Yah to govern the existence of man on earth to what Christianity offers as an alternative, it becomes extremely clear that there can be no replacement of these eternal values.

Holy Scriptures Moral & Civil Laws

Exodus 20:7-14
Thou shalt not take the name of the Lord thy God in vain; for the Lord will not hold him guiltless that taketh His name in vain. Remember the Sabbath day, to keep it holy. Six days shalt thou labor, and do all thy work; but the seventh day is a Sabbath unto the Lord thy God, in it thou shalt not do any manner of work, thou, nor thy son, nor thy daughter, nor thy man-servant, nor thy maid-servant, nor thy cattle, nor thy stranger that is within thy gates; for in six days the Lord made heaven and earth, the sea, and all that in them is, and rested on the seventh day; wherefore the

New Testament Moral Civil Teachings

1 Corinthians 7:25-40
Now, concerning what you wrote about unmarried people: I do not have a command from the Lord, but I give my opinion as one who is by the Lord's mercy who is worthy of trust. Considering the present distress, I think it is better for a man to stay as he is. Do you have a wife? Then don't try to get rid of her. Are you unmarried? Then don't look for a wife. But if you do marry, you haven't committed a sin. But I would rather spare you the everyday troubles that married people will have. What I mean, my brothers, is this: there is not much time left, and from now on

Lord blessed the Sabbath day, and hallowed it. Honor thy father and thy mother, that thy days may be long upon the land which the Lord thy God giveth thee. Thou shalt not murder. Thou shalt not commit adultery. Thou shalt not steal. Thou shalt not bear false witness against thy neighbor. Thou shalt not covet thy neighbor's house; thou shalt not covet thy neighbor's wife, nor his man-servant, nor his maid-servant, nor his ox, nor his ass, nor anything that is thy neighbor's.

Leviticus 19:11-19
Ye shall not steal; neither shall ye deal falsely, nor lie one to another. And ye shall not swear by My name falsely, so that thou profane the name of thy God; I am the Lord. Thou shall not oppress thy neighbor, nor rob him; the wages of a hired servant shall not abide with thee all night until the morning. Thou shalt not curse the deaf, nor put a stumbling-block before the blind, but thou shalt fear thy God: I am the Lord. Ye shall do no unrighteousness in judgment; thou shalt not respect the person of the poor, nor favor the person of the mighty; but in righteousness shalt thou judge thy

married men should live as though they were not married; those who weep, as though they were not sad; those who laugh, as though they were not happy; those who buy, as though they did not own what they bought; those who deal in material goods, as though they were not fully occupied with them. For this world, as it is now, will not last much longer. I would like you to be free from worry. An unmarried man concerns himself with the Lord's work, because he is trying to please the Lord.

1 Corinthians 11:1-14
Imitate me, then, just as I imitate Christ. I praise you because you always remember me and follow the teachings that I have handed on to you. But I want you to understand that Christ is the supreme over every man, the husband is supreme over the wife, and God is the supreme over Christ. So a man who proclaims God's message in public worship with nothing on her head disgraces her husband; there is no difference between her and a woman whose head has been shaved. If the woman does not cover her head, she

neighbor. Thou shalt not go up and down as a talebearer among thy people; neither shalt thou stand idly by the blood of thy neighbor: I am the Lord. Thou shalt not hate thy neighbor in thy heart; thou shalt surely rebuke thy neighbor, and not bear sin because of him. Thou shalt not take vengeance, nor bear any grudge against the children of thy people, but thou shalt love thy neighbor as thyself: I am the Lord. Ye shalt keep My statutes. Thou shalt not let thy cattle gender with a diverse kind; thou shalt not sow thy field with two kinds of seeds; neither shall there come upon you a garment of two kinds of stuff mingled together.

Exodus 23:1-5
Thou shalt not utter a false report; put not thy hand with the wicked to be an unrighteous witness. Thou shalt not follow a multitude to do evil; neither shalt thou bear witness in a cause to turn aside after a multitude to pervert justice; neither shalt thou favor a poor man in his cause. If thy meet thy enemy's ox or his ass going astray, thou shalt surely bring it back to him again. If thy see the ass of him that hateth thee lying under its

might as well cut her hair. A man has no need to cover his head, because he reflects the image and glory of God. But woman reflects the glory of man; for man was not created from woman, but woman from man. Nor was man created for woman's sake, but woman was created for man's sake. On account of the angels, then, a woman should have a covering over her head to show that she is under her husband's authority. In our life in the Lord, however, woman is not independent of man, nor is man independent of woman. For as woman was made from man, in the same way is man born from woman; and it is God who brings everything into existence. Judge for yourselves whether it is proper for a woman to pray to God in public worship with nothing on her head. Why, nature itself teaches you that long hair on a man is a disgrace, but on a woman it is a thing of beauty.

Corinthians 13:13
Meanwhile these three remain: faith, hope, and love; and the greatest of these is love.

burden, thou shalt forbear to pass with him; thou shalt surely release it with him.

Deuteronomy 22:5-19
A woman shall not wear that which pretaineth to a man, neither shall a man put on a woman's garment; for whosoever doeth these things is an abomination unto the Lord thy God. If a bird's nest chance to be before thee in the way, in any tree or on the ground, with young ones or eggs, and the dam sitting upon the young, or upon the eggs, thou shalt not take the dam with the young; thou shalt in any wise let the dam go, but the young thou mayest take unto thyself; that it may be well with thee, and that thou mayest prolong thy days. When thou buildest a new house, then thou shalt make a parapet for thy roof, that thou bringest not blood upon thy house, if any man fall from thence. Thou shalt not sow thy vineyard with two kinds of seeds; lest the fullness of the seed which thou hast sown be forfeited together with the increase of the vineyard. Thou shalt not plow with an ox and an ass together. Thou shalt not wear a mingled stuff, wool and

Romans 9:14-25
Shall we say, then, that God is unjust? Not at all. For he said to Moses, "I will have mercy on anyone I wish; I will take pity on anyone I wish." So then, everything depends, not on what man wants or does, but only on God's mercy. For the scripture says to the king of Egypt, "I made you king in order to use you to show my power and to spread my fame over the whole world." So then, God has mercy on anyone he wishes, and he makes stubborn anyone he wishes. But one of you will say to me, "If this is so, how can God find fault with anyone? Who can resist God's will?" But who are you, my friend, to talk back to God? A clay pot does not ask the man who made it, "Why did you make me like this?" After all, the man who makes the pots has a right to use the clay as he wishes, and to make two pots from the same lump of clay, one for special occasions and the other for ordinary use. And the same is true for what God has done. He wanted to show his anger and to make his power known. But he was very patient in enduring

linen together. Thou shalt make thee twisted cords upon the four corners of thy covering, wherewith thy covereth thyself. If any man take a wife, and go inn unto her, and hate her, and lay wanton charges against her, and say: 'I took this woman, and when I came nigh to her, I found not in her the tokens of virginity'; then shall the father of the damsel, and her mother, take and bring forth the tokens of the damsel's virginity unto the elders of the city in the gate. And the damsel's father shall say unto the elders: 'I gave my daughter unto this man to wife, and he hateth her; and, lo, he hath laid wanton charges, saying: I found not in thy daughter the tokens of virginity; and yet these are the tokens of my daughter's virginity.' And they shalt spread the garment before the elders of the city. And the elders of that city shall take the man and chastise him. And they shall fine him a hundred shekels of silver, and give them unto the father of the damsel, because he had brought up an evil name upon a virgin of Israel; and she shall be his wife; he may not put her away all his days.

those who were the objects o his anger, who were doomed to destruction. And he also wanted to reveal his abundant glory, which was poured out on us who were the objects of his mercy, those of us whom he has prepared to receive his glory. For we are the people he called, not only from among the Jews but also from among the Gentiles. This is what he says in the book of Hosea: "The people who were not mine I will call 'My People.' The nation that I did not love I will call 'My Beloved.'

There are literally no laws in the New Testament which are orginally from Yah. Therefore it is no surprise the list presented would be so short.

Numbers 15:37-41
And the Lord spoke unto Moses, saying: 'Speak unto the children of Israel, and bid them that they make them throughout their generations fringes in the corners of their garments, and that they put with the fringe of each corner a thread of blue. And it shall be unto you for a fringe, that ye may look upon it, and remember all the commandments of the Lord, and do them; and that ye go not about after your own heart and your own eyes, after which ye use to go astray; that ye may remember and do all My commandments, and be holy unto your God. I am the Lord thy God, who brought you out of the land of Egypt, to be your God: I am the Lord your God.

Exodus 21:12-20
He that smiteth a man, so that he dieth, shall surely be put to death. And if a man lie not in wait, but God cause it to come to hand; then I will appoint thee a place whither he may flee. And if a man come presumptuously upon his neighbor, to slay him with guile; thou shall take him from Mine altar, that he may die. And he that smiteth his father, or his mother, shall be

surely put to death. And he that stealeth a man, and selleth him, or if he be found in his hand, he shall surely be put to death. And if men contend, and one smite the other with a stone, or with his fist, and he die not, but keep his bed; if he rise again, and walk abroad upon his staff, then shall he that smote him be quit; only he shall pay for the loss of his time, and shall cause him to be thoroughly healed. And if a man smite his bondman, or his bondwoman, with a rod, and he die under his hand, he shall surely be punished.

Exodus 22:4-26
If a man cause a field or vineyard to be eaten, and shall let his beast loose, and it feed in another man's field; of the best of his own field, and of the best of his own vineyard, shall he make restitution. If fire break out, and catch in thorns, so that the shocks of corn, or the standing corn, or the field are consumed; he that kindled the fire shall surely make restitution. If a man deliver unto his neighbor money or stuff to keep, and it be stolen out of the man's house; if the thief be found, he shall pay double. If the thief be not found, then the

master of the house shall come near unto God and, to see whither he have not put his hand unto his neighbor's goods. For every matter of trespass, whether it be for ox, for ass, for sheep, for raiment, or for any manner of lost thing, whereof one saith: 'This is it,' the cause of both parties shall come before God; he whom God shall condemn shall pay double unto his neighbor. If a man deliver onto his neighbor an ass, or an ox, or a sheep, or any beast, to keep, and it die, or be hurt, or driven away, no man seeth it. Then shall an oath of the LORD be between them both, that he hath not put his hand unto his neighbour's goods; and the owner of it shall accept thereof, and he shall not make it good.And if it be stolen from him, he shall make restitution unto the owner thereof. If it be torn in pieces, then let him bring it for witness, and he shall not make good that which was torn. And if a man borrow ought of his neighbour, and it be hurt, or die, the owner thereof being not with it, he shall surely make it good. But if the owner thereof be with it, he shall not make it good: if it be an hired thing, it came for his hire. And if a man entice a maid that is not betrothed, and lie with her, he shall surely endow her to be his wife. If her father utterly refuse to give her unto him, he shall pay money according to the dowry of virgins. Thou shalt not suffer a witch to live. Whosoever lieth with a beast shall surely be put to death. He that sacrificeth unto any god, save unto the LORD only, he shall be utterly destroyed. Thou shalt neither vex a stranger, nor oppress him: for ye were strangers in the land of Egypt. Ye shall not afflict any widow, or fatherless child. If thou afflict them in any wise, and they cry at all unto me, I will surely hear their cry; And my wrath shall wax hot, and I will kill you with the sword; and your wives shall be widows, and your children fatherless. If thou lend money to any of my people that is poor by thee, thou shalt not be to him as an usurer, neither shalt thou lay upon him usury. If thou at all take thy neighbour's raiment to pledge, thou shalt deliver it unto him by that the sun goeth down: For that is his covering only, it is his raiment for his skin: wherein shall he sleep? and it shall come to pass, when he crieth unto me, that I will hear; for I am gracious.

THE LAWS OF UNCLEANLINESS

The laws of uncleanliness are instructions from the Creator in the form of rules. They represent a sanitary and dietary standard of behavior designed to insure the health and sanctity of Israel.

Israel's diet, originally established in the Garden of Eden, was established as a vegan diet, Genesis 1:29. Since that time however, animals, which were permitted by law for consumption, were placed under a classification of three characteristics. All animals, which do not have all three characteristics, were forbidden in dietary consumption. Fish and all other swarming things in the waters are another example where law of uncleanness must be adhered. Crustaceans and anything which swarms the waters without fins and scales is unclean. These creatures are like the swine of the earth, they are unclean because they are scavengers.

Many present day diseases are attributed to diet. A great number of these sicknesses which plague mankind doctors identify flesh (meat) consumption as a direct cause. Mad cow disease and hoof and mouth disease have caused many intelligent people to reconsider their diet. On the other hand, diabetes, high blood pressure, breast cancer, and prostate cancer have forced millions to abandon poor eating habits.

Men and women may acquire uncleannesses. Sexually transmitted diseases, which may also cause a flow or stoppage of body fluids, are uncleanness. Diseases such as gonorrhea, syphilis and herpes are a few examples.

Whenever a female has an issue of blood which flows such as the monthly menstruation, she is unclean. Following childbirth a woman is unclean forty days for the birth of a son and unclean eighty days if she gives birth to a daughter. A flow of blood from a male is also a cause of uncleanness. All uncleaness holds a primary significance where holiness and the sanctuary of the Creator exist. The home, community and environment had to be free of bacteria or fungus, which could form leprosy. Related plagues could affect garments, vessels and buildings made of wood or brick.

While all this and more evidence exist about laws and practices in the Old Testament, there is nothing in the New Testament which comes close to practices which are considered original laws. Once again, a comparative study reveals that when it comes to laws of the Bible there are virtually no laws given by the Creator in the New Testaments. The laws of the Creator are only found in the Old Testament. Because Christianity is a religion of custom and practices from a wide range of areas and cultures it has no original laws or practices of its own. Whenever culture does not exist, there can be no existence of a people.

Holy Scriptures Clean & Unclean Dietary

Genesis 1:29-31
And God said: 'Behold, I have given you every herb yielding seed, which is upon the face of all the earth, and every tree, in which is the fruit of a tree yielding seed- to you it shall be for food; and to every beast of the earth, and to every fowl of the air, and to everything that creepeth upon the earth, wherein there is a living soul, [I have given] every green herb for food.' And it was so. And God saw everything that He had made, and, behold it was very good. And there was evening and there was morning, the sixth day.

New Testament Dietary Teachings

Acts 10:9-15
The next day, as they were on their way and coming near Joppa, Peter went up on the house about noon in order to pray. He became hungry and wanted something to eat; while the food was being prepared, he had a vision. He saw heaven opened and something coming down that looked like a large sheet being lowered by its four corners to the earth. In it were all kinds of animals, reptiles, and wild birds. A voice said to him, "Get up, Peter; kill and eat!" But Peter said, "Certainly not, Lord! I have never eaten anything ritually unclean or defiled." The voice spoke to him again, "Do not consider anything unclean that God has declared clean."

Leviticus 11:1-7
And the Lord spoke unto Moses and to Aaron, saying unto them: Speak unto the children of Israel, saying: These are the living things which ye may eat among all the beasts that are on the earth. Whatsoever parteth the hoof, and is wholly cloven-footed, and cheweth the cud, among the beasts, that may ye eat. Nevertheless these may ye not eat of them that only chew the cud, or of them that only part the hoof: the camel, because he cheweth the cud but parteth not the hoof, he is unclean unto you. And the rock-badger, because he cheweth the cud but parteth not the hoof, he is unclean unto you. And the hare, because she cheweth the cud but parteth not the hoof, she is unclean unto you. And the swine, because he parteth the hoof, and is cloven-footed, but cheweth not the cud, he is unclean unto you.

Deuteronomy 14:9-20
These ye may eat of all that is in the waters: whatsoever hath fins and scales may ye eat; and whatsoever hath not fins and scales ye shall not eat; it is

1 Corinthians 8:1-12
Now, concerning what you wrote about food offered to idols. It is true, of course, that "all of us have knowledge," as they say. Such knowledge, however, puffs a person up with pride; but loves builds up. Whoever thinks he knows something really doesn't know as he ought to know. But the person who loves God is known by him. So then, about eating the food offered to idols: we know that a idol stand for something that does not really exist; we know that there is only the one God, the Father, who is the Creator of all things and for whom we live; and there is only one Lord, Jesus Christ, through whom all things were created and through whom we live. But everyone knows this truth. Some people have been so used to idols that to this day when they eat such food they still think of it as food that belongs to an idol; their conscience is weak, and they feel they are defiled by the food. Food, however, will not improve our relation with God; we shall not lose anything if we do not eat, nor shall we gain anything if we do eat. Be careful, however,

unclean unto you. Of all clean birds ye may eat. But these are they which ye may not eat: the great vulture, and the bearded vulture, and the ospray; and the glede, and the falcon, and the kite after its kinds; and every raven after its kinds; and the ostrich, and the night-hawk, and the sea-mew, and the hawk after its kinds; the little owl, and the great owl, and the horned owl; and the pelican, and the carrion-vulture, and the cormorant; and the stork, and the heron after its kinds, and the hoopoe, and the bat. And all winged swarming things are unclean unto you; they shall not be eaten. Of all clean winged things ye may eat.

not to let your freedom of action make those who are weak in the faith fall into sin. Suppose a person whose conscience is weak in this matter sees you, who have so-called "knowledge," eating in the temple of an idol; will not this encourage him to eat food offered to idols? And so this weak person, your brother for whom Christ died, will perish because of your "knowledge"! And in this way you will be sinning against Christ by sinning against your Christian brothers and wounding their weak conscience. So then, if food makes my brother sin, I will never eat meat again, so as not to make my brother fall into sin.

Genesis 9:3-5
Every moving thing that liveth shall be for food for you; as the green herb have I given you all. Only flesh with the life thereof, which is the blood thereof, shall ye not eat. And surely your blood of your lives will I require; at the hand of every beasts will I require it; and at the hand of man, even at the hand of every man's brother, will I require the life of man.

Holy Scripture Uncleanliness

Leviticus 13:1-3
And the Lord spoke unto Moses and unto Aaron, saying: When a man shall have in the skin of his flesh a rising, or a scab, or a bright spot, and it become in the skin of his flesh the plague of leprosy, then he shall be brought unto Aaron the priest, or unto one of his sons the priests. And the priest shall look upon the plague in the skin of the flesh; and if the hair in the plague be turned white, and the appearance of the plague be deeper than the skin of his flesh, it is the plague of leprosy; and the priest shall look upon him, and pronounce him unclean.

Leviticus 14:19-20
And the priest shall offer the sin-offering, and make atonement for him that is to be cleansed because of his uncleanness; and afterward he shall kill the burnt-offering. And the priest shall offer the burnt-offering and the meal-offering upon the altar; and the priest shall make atonement for him, and he shall be clean.

New Testament Uncleanliness

There are no uncleanesses mentioned in the New Testament, which are similar to the Laws found in the Old Testament. However, the New testament does mention of unclean spirits and devils possessing human bodies.

Leviticus 15:1-3

And the Lord spoke unto Moses and to Aaron, saying: Speak unto the children of Israel, and say unto them: When any man hath an issue out of his flesh, his issue is unclean. And this shall be his uncleanness in his issue: whether his flesh run with his issue, or his flesh be stopped from his issue, it is his uncleanness.

Leviticus 12:1-6

And the Lord spoke unto Moses, saying: Speak unto the children of Israel, saying: If a woman be delivered, and bear a man-child, then she shall be unclean seven days; as in the days of the impurity of her sickness shall she be unclean. And in the eight day the flesh of his foreskin shall be circumcised. And she shall continue in the blood of purification three and thirty days; she shall touch no hallowed thing, nor come into the sanctuary, until the days of her purification be fulfilled. But if she bear a maid-child, then she shall be unclean two weeks, as in her impurity; and she shall continue in the blood of purification threescore and six days. And when the days of her purification are fulfilled, for a son, or for a daughter, she shall bring a lamb of the first year for a burnt-offering, and a young pigeon, or a turtle-dove, for a sin-offering, unto the door of the tent of meeting, unto the priest.

Leviticus 15:16-18
And if the flow of seed go out from a man, then he shall bathe all his flesh in water, and be unclean until the even. And every garment, and every skin, whereon is the flow of seed, shall be washed with water, and be unclean until the even. The woman also with whom a man shall lie carnally, they shall both bathe themselves in water, and be unclean until the even.

Leviticus 15:19-24
And if a woman have an issue, and her issue in her flesh be blood, she shall be in her impurity seven days; and whosoever toucheth her shall be unclean until the even. And everything that she lieth upon in her impurity shall be unclean; everything also that she sitteth upon shall be unclean. And whoever toucheth her bed shall

wash his clothes, and bathe himself in water, and shall be unclean until the even. And whosoever toucheth any thing that she sitteth upon shall wash his clothes, and bathe himself in water, and be unclean until the even. And if he be on the bed, or on any thing whereon she sitteth, when he toucheth it, he shall be unclean until the even. And if any man lie with her, and her impurity be upon him, he shall be unclean seven days; and every bed whereon he lieth shall be unclean.

Unfortunately, due to the teachings of Paul many innocent souls have been led astray from the law because they view the Bible as being the entire word of God. In some ways it is understandable why people have been deceived when we read precepts like Ephesians 2:1-9 another epistle written by Paul who alleges that people are save by grace through faith in Christ Jesus.

> *But that no man is justified by the law in the sight of God, it is evident: for, The just shall live by faith.*
>
> *And the law is not of faith: but, The man that doeth them shall live in them.*
>
> *Christ hath redeemed us from the curse of the law, being made a curse for us: for it is written, Cursed is every one that hangeth on a tree:*
>
> *That the blessing of Abraham might come on the Gentiles through Jesus Christ; that we might receive the promise of the Spirit through faith.*
>
> *Brethren, I speak after the manner of men; Though it be but a man's covenant, yet if it be confirmed, no*

man disannulleth, or addeth thereto.

Now to Abraham and his seed were the promises made. He saith not, And to seeds, as of many; but as of one, And to thy seed, which is Christ.

And this I say, that the covenant, that was confirmed before of God in Christ, the law, which was four hundred and thirty years after, cannot disannul, that it should make the promise of none effect.

For if the inheritance be of the law, it is no more of promise: but God gave it to Abraham by promise.

Wherefore then serveth the law? It was added because of transgressions, till the seed should come to whom the promise was made; and it was ordained by angels in the hand of a mediator.

Now a mediator is not a mediator of one, but God is one.

Is the law then against the promises of God? God forbid: for if there had been a law given which could have given life, verily righteousness should have been by the law.

Galatians 3:11-21

How can the Greek writings say on one hand that "not one jot nor one tittle shall be removed from the Law until heaven and earth pass away" and on the other hand, say "the Law has been done away with?" The source of their own doctrine in the Greek Writings in Matthew 5:17-20 further states that:

"He who breaks the least of these commandments or teaches others to do so shall be least in the Kingdom of GOD.

Think not that I am come to destroy the law, or the prophets: I am not come to destroy, but to fulfill.

> *For verily I say unto you, Till heaven and earth pass, one jot or one tittle shall in no wise pass from the law, till all be fulfilled.*
>
> *Whosoever therefore shall break one of these least commandments, and shall teach men so, he shall be called the least in the kingdom of heaven: but whosoever shall do and teach them, the same shall be called great in the kingdom of heaven."*

Those who compiled the New Testament had to know the truth recorded in the Holy scriptures and deliberately lied to support the Christian doctrine.

However, Isaiah uses few words to set the record straight concerning the law.

> *To the law and to the testimony: if they speak not according to this word, it is because there is no light in them.*
>
> ***Isaiah 8:20***

> *Let us hear the conclusion of the whole matter: Fear God, and keep his commandments: for this is the whole duty of man.*
>
> *For God shall bring every work into judgment, with every secret thing, whether it be good, or whether it be evil.*
>
> ***Ecclesiastes 12:13-14***

INACCURATE TRANSLATIONS, FALSE INTERPRETATIONS AND DISCREPANCIES

For the thousands of people familiar with the debate as to whether or not Jesus is mentioned in the Old Testament scriptures, and whether or not he is the reference figure of numerous precepts cited in the Bible, will agree that Isaiah 53 is one of the most frequently used chapters, quoted by Christians making this assertion.

Yet, just as with many other false assertions, this particular claim has been made without any regard to the historical nature of the Bible. Each, book, and the subsequent scriptures that make up each book, occured at specific points of time. Therefore, one must know the Bible as it presents itself beginning in Genesis with a clear understanding of the Holy Scripture's account of the people of Israel's history. If the New Testament is read, it can only be read and understood where it is in harmony with the history and authority of the Old Testament. Again, far from it being a religious book, the Bible is the historical account of the Children of Israel, their particular relationship with their Creator, Yahwah, and their relationships with the various other peoples of the world, both in antiquity and into the future.

The proper understanding of any quote from the Old Testament is only possible when one takes into account the political and social climate at that particular point of time. The Prophet Isaiah, for instance, begins his account "concerning Judah and Jerusalem, in the days of Uzziah, Jotham, Ahaz, and Hezekiah-kings of Judah." (Isaiah 1:1-66)

The original Hebrew text of Isaiah was a scroll without numerated chapters as we know them. Yet each episode builds upon the history of the chapter that preceded. The unfolding of the historical narrative follows a precise timeline. The idea that Isaiah 53 is somehow independent of the rest of the book of Isaiah, and for that matter, the rest of the historical narratives that precede it, is nonsensical. If we begin reading at Isaiah Chapter 52 straight through Isaiah Chapter 53, and it will be transparent that there is absolutely no reference or connection to Jesus, the Christian personality of the New Testament.

As a spokesman for Yahwah, Isaiah 52:1-6 commands the people of Jerusalem to awake and take a dignified stand. It is important to understand that at this time the inhabitants of Jerusalem were mainly of the tribe of Judah with small portions of the Levite and Benjamite families among them. Also, at the time of this prophecy, the Northern Kingdom of Israel made up of the remaining ten tribes had already fallen into the hand of Assyrian oppression.

> *Awake, awake; put on thy strength, O Zion; put on thy beautiful garments, O Jerusalem, the holy city: for henceforth there shall no more come into thee the uncircumcised and the unclean.*
>
> *Shake thyself from the dust; arise, and sit down, O Jerusalem: loose thyself from the bands of thy neck, O captive daughter of Zion.*
>
> *For thus saith the Lord, Ye have sold yourselves for naught; and ye shall be redeemed without money.*
>
> *For thus saith the Lord God, My people went down formerly into Egypt to sojourn there; and the Assyrian oppressed them without cause.*
>
> *Now therefore, what have I here, saith the Lord, that my people is taken away for naught? they that rule over them make them to howl, saith the Lord; and my name continually every day is blasphemed.*
>
> *Therefore my people shall know my name: therefore they shall know in that day that I am he that doth speak: behold, it is I.*

The prophetic vision of Isaiah, here envisions the rise of Babylonians as those oppressors selected by Yah to oppress those in Jerusalem. Nonetheless, in the finale Isaiah is the messenger of good tidings in his announcement that salvation and redemption will come through their God, (יהוה). Who reigneth!

> *How beautiful upon the mountains are the feet of him that bringeth good tidings, that publisheth peace; that bringeth good tidings of good, that publisheth salvation; that saith unto Zion, Thy God reigneth!*
>
> *Thy watchmen shall lift up the voice; with the voice together shall they sing: for they shall see eye to eye, when the Lord shall bring again Zion.*
>
> *Break forth into joy, sing together, ye waste places of Jerusalem: for the Lord hath comforted his people, he hath redeemed Jerusalem.*
>
> *The Lord hath made bare his holy arm in the eyes of all the nations; and all the ends of the earth shall see the salvation of our God.*
>
> *Depart ye, depart ye, go ye out from thence, touch no unclean thing; go ye out of the midst of her; be ye clean, that bear the vessels of the Lord.*
>
> *For ye shall not go out with haste, nor go by flight: for the Lord will go before you; and the God of Israel will be your rearward.*
>
> ***Isaiah 52:7-12***

Isaiah 52:13-15 immediately precedes Isaiah 53. It is here, where the identification of the subject spoken about has to be clear, because as we continue into Isaiah 53 the subject is unidentified by name. The 53rd chapter can only be properly understood by reading the chapters which preceded it. The subject is mentioned specifically by the name Israel and not by a third person pronoun.

> *Behold, my servant shall deal prudently, he shall be exalted and extolled, and be very high.*

As many were astonished at thee; his visage was so marred more than any man, and his form more than the sons of men:

So shall he startle many nations; the kings shall shut their mouths at him: for that which had not been told them shall they see; and that which they had not heard shall they consider.

This chapter deals with the prophet's message to Israel concerning their plummet from riches to rags. As a result of Israel's fall from grace in the sight of their Creator, it is now questionable about who would believe their report and the fact that God has revealed His doings unto them. The prophet Isaiah is careful to point out how Israel and the nations of the world have suffered due to Israel's neglect and refusal to obey and teach God's Law. Key phrases such as *"my servant, His people unto whom the stroke was due"*, and numerous references to the subject Israel in the plural sense, strenghtens the position that Isaiah was referring to his people Israel and not making any future reference to a promised "savior."

The pronouns within this chapter and the ambiguous manner in which the prophet speaks about Israel has led some to believe that they can force Jesus in this passage to support their claims. However, under close examination this is easily proven to be false. The contents and context of the entire book of Isaiah, and certainly the chapters immediately before and after Isaiah 53, indicate that the only reference that can be made is to the people of Israel.

In fact, this is the format of Isaiah's entire discourse in the 53rd chapter. His use of the first person – singular, third person, – singular, and third person, and first person – plural pronouns are interchangeable whenever he identifies the subject of the Nation of Israel of which he writes. There is absolutely no thought or reference to Jesus. Isaiah repeatedly speaks of this subject the Nation of Israel in the third person – singular and first person – plural which in those instances is inclusive of himself. At other times Isaiah wrote as an external party. Verse two says, *"For he shot up right forth as a sampling, and as a root out of a dry ground, he had no form nor comeliness, that we should look upon him, nor beauty that we should delight in him."*

Simply because certain ideas are expressed about someone being despised, led to slaughter, bruised, crushed and accepted the suffering and pain without protest, does not mean it was Jesus. In fact all of the above happened to the people of Israel. Also, merely because a sentence or phrase is expressed in an ambiguous manner there is no reason without evidence to suggest it refers to Jesus. In most instances the sentence or phrase is made clear in a paragraph or the chapter.

The usage of this metaphor describes the humble beginning and manner in which Israel sprang up among the nations. A metaphor is a figure speech in which a word or phrase literally denoting one kind of object or idea is used in place of another to suggest a likeness or analogy between them. Whenever a person is reading any kind of literature, they must have solid reading skills. Basic reading skills are essential to any reading process. There is no exception when it comes to the Bible. In fact, the more difficult the reading material, the greater the skill required for comprehension

Israel was chosen because God loved them and saw that they were fewest among the nations See the passage found in Deuteronomy below. They rose from a few nomadic sojourners in the land of Canaan to become a Holy people numbering well over a million people at the time of their Exodus from Egypt land.

> *The Lord did not set his love upon you, nor choose you, because ye were more in number than any people; for ye were the fewest of all people:*
>
> *But because the Lord loved you, and because he would keep the oath which he had sworn unto your fathers, hath the Lord brought you out with a mighty hand, and redeemed you out of the house of bondmen, from the hand of Pharaoh king of Egypt.*
>
> *Know therefore that the Lord thy God, he is God, the faithful God, which keepeth covenant and mercy with*

them that love him and keep his commandments to a thousand generations;

And repayeth them that hate him to their face, to destroy them: he will not be slack to him that hateth him, he will repay him to his face.

Thou shalt therefore keep the commandments, and the statutes, and the judgments, which I command thee this day, to do them.

Deuteronomy 7:7-11

Israel's enslavement under cruel bondage in Egypt speaks to the low esteem afforded them by the nations. It also explains why Isaiah describes them as having no national form or attractiveness or beauty that the nations of the world should delight in their historical experience. Verse 3 in Isaiah 53 reads "***he is despised, and rejected of men, a man of sorrows,*** *and acquainted with grief, an as one from which men hide their face. " He was despised, and we esteemed him not.*" "My servant" refers to the Nation of Israel. Israel is of whom the pronoun "he" is referring to. In other words, Yahwah is proclaiming through the mouth of Isaiah that Israel's repeated association with troubled times and affliction became a source of historical shame. There was a great dread in Israel of the many diseases of Egypt of which they were well acquainted. Leprosy, for instance, became a dreaded disease after the Exodus from Egypt. Isaiah's literary privilege is illustrated because Yahwah allows him to shift himself as the writer to exclude himself when he expresses God's view of how Israel is perceived by the foreign nations. As a result, Isaiah writes "we" esteemed Him not.

In verse 4 he continues in this train of thought. *"Surely our diseases he did bear, and our pains he carried, whereas we did esteem him stricken, smitten of God and afflicted."* It can only be a foreign viewpoint expressed in verse 4. Isaiah 43:6 reads *"I the Lord Yah have called thee in righteousness, and have taken hold of thy hand, and kept thee, and set thee for a covenant of the people, for a light of nations."* This is the proper connection made by Isaiah to the Divine purpose of the "Holy people" chosen by Yah. Israel was given the responsibility of being a light or source of truth unto the nations of the world.

Their disobedience became a source of guilt for what has happened among the foreign nations in regard to their lack of knowledge about the true God of the universe and His righteous laws. Consequently, what has happened to Israel or Blacks in the Diaspora is a punishment for their failure to obey God's laws. (Deuteronomy 28:15-68). Notwithstanding, the global role Israel is to play in the restoration of truth is more important than the national humiliation God has wrought in afflicting them. Their punishment metaphorically described as the "wounds" of a third person, male is attributed to transgressions committed by the nations due to Israel's failure to represent God as a righteous people not Jesus.

The welfare of all nations in the future is also a reason for the chastisement of Israel. Their national experience will ultimately serve as a historical reference and a source of healing for the nations in their restoration. This is the background to the verse which says, *"But he was wounded because of our transgressions, he was crushed because of our iniquities. The chastisement of our welfare was upon him and with his stripes we were healed."*

The Hebrew scriptures were written using metaphor, simile and other figurative language which often depicts the Nation of Israel as sheep who have disobeyed and strayed from the righteous path set before them. As a result, the sins of the entire world rest on the shoulders of Israel "the chosen people."

The 53rd chapter is just one example of the various different references to Israel as a collective as well as an individual. The various tribulations, chastisements and salvation directed at Israel because of their peculiar portion as a savior nation was due to the responsibility they had to Yah's Laws.

If the Bible is simply viewed as a series of mini Bible stories, based upon some religiously assigned viewpoint, or as isolated chapters and/or precepts, the reader will fail to understand it. It is significant to note that

Isaiah lived during the period (765-696 BCE) and witnessed the Assyrian Empire rise to power. Jeremiah lived during the period 600 BCE and witnessed the Babylonian invasion into the Holy Land. Indeed, Jeremiah became a victim suffering great anguish at the hands of his own people for prophesying about the assured victory of the Babylonians against Israel. King Zedekiah and the princes of Judah treated his words as treachery and traitorous. Ezekiel, a Priest and Prophet was taken captive to Babylon. Daniel was a youth among the captives chosen to serve in Nebuchadnezzar's court in Babylon. Some Prophets were contemporaries. For example, Isaiah and Micah were contemporaries although decades separated their ages.

The books of the Prophet Zechariah, Haggai, Nehemiah and Ezra, Habbukuk, Joel, Zephaniah all concern themselves with the years following the Babylonian captivity and the return to the Holy Land in the years of Darius and Cyrus who permitted the rebuilding the Second Temple. Malachi is reportedly the last of the Hebrew Prophets. He ended the line of Inspired Prophets. Afterwards there were no words spoken or revealed from Yah to His chosen people. The decree to scatter Israel to the four corners of the earth was manifested. At that point, the books were closed and the writings were sealed.

> *And the vision of all is become unto you as the words of a book that is sealed, which men deliver to one that is learned, saying, Read this, I pray thee: and he saith, I cannot; for it is sealed:*
>
> *And the book is delivered to him that is not learned, saying, Read this, I pray thee: and he saith, I am not learned.*
>
> ***Isaiah 29: 11-12***

The defiled Nation of Israel entered into a gradual mental and spiritual sleep among the nations of the world. Consequently, a deep darkness was cast over the Holy Scriptures, and a blanket of ignorance over the people by their Creator. The revelation can only be witnessed in the historical experience of the Black Man. Their state of mind and their condition corroborates these facts. Shame, confusion and oppression in the land of their captors was the decree of their God, Yahwah. Subsequently other nations were deprived of the light of Truth. As a result, there has been a misrepresentation of the facts in Christian teachings. Namely, the ideas which purports the birth, life and death of Jesus is some sort of escape, redemption from the declarations of the Almighty spoken by the mouth of the Prophets in the Holy Scriptures. Bible scholarship will show that prophecy in the Holy Scriptures or Old Testament differs considerably from the alleged vision of John in the book of Revelations. There are only four books in the New Testament which represent history, Matthew, Mark, Luke and John. The fact that they have varied accounts of the same events has created much skepticism and discussion among scholars. The book of Acts of the Apostles outline the events which followed the death of Jesus. The Epistles are simply the letters written by Paul and others to mostly Gentile people who converted to Christianity. These were personal letters which expressed some of Paul's personal opinions or views which he shared with those converts. Many of Paul's opinions and personal views contradict what Jesus said and more importantly the words in the Law of Almighty Yah.

Ironically, Jesus did not write a single book. All accounts attributed to him were recorded decades or centuries after his death. Therefore, where does the authority behind any instruction within the Greek writings of the New Testament rest? Nowhere. It is a grave mistake when an individual believes that Yahwah inspired messages in the Greek writings/New Testament. It is also a wrong assumption to think that there is any connection or transition between Hebrew Inspired Prophets and Greek scribes based upon a common Truth from Yahwah. The wisest step toward making a separation of the Truth and a lie in the Bible begins with a return to the Holy Scriptures. The Old Testament alone must be recognized as the foundation and authority for true understanding and application of the Creator's words. The Holy Scriptures or Old Testament must be given precedence in it's authority for Truth over and above the Greek writings or New Testament.

In understanding the Holy Scriptures it is essential to recognize that the Torah or five Books of Moses takes precedence over the prophecy.

The Prophets came to Israel to admonish them for their rejection of the Law. No Prophet came with instruction to break or change the Law. Violation of the Law was the source of the problem in biblical times within the Nation of Israel. The Torah or Law was the foundation of all instruction to Israel in the Bible. Therefore, the books of Genesis, Exodus, Leviticus, Numbers and Deuteronomy must be read and understood initially in Bible study.

First and foremost, the New Testament is not a document which benefits anyone who seeks to serve and obey the Most High Yah. Israelites who adhere to it's false instruction are in violation of the Law. There is no escape from this fact. Those who are Christians or foreigners of other nations should seek their Creator and keep His laws. The Creator who chose Israel is also the Creator of all people. The Creator's Law will one day be acknowledged and kept by all nations.

> *Thus saith the LORD, Keep ye judgment, and do justice: for my salvation is near to come, and my righteousness to be revealed.*
>
> *Blessed is the man that doeth this, and the son of man that layeth hold on it; that keepeth the sabbath from polluting it, and keepeth his hand from doing any evil.*
>
> *Neither let the son of the stranger, that hath joined himself to the LORD, speak, saying, The LORD hath utterly separated me from his people: neither let the eunuch say, Behold, I am a dry tree.*
>
> *For thus saith the LORD unto the eunuchs that keep my sabbaths, and choose the things that please me, and take hold of my covenant;*
>
> *Even unto them will I give in mine house and within my walls a place and a name better than of sons and of daughters: I will give them an everlasting name, that shall not be cut off.*

> *Also the sons of the stranger, that join themselves to the LORD, to serve him, and to love the name of the LORD, to be his servants, every one that keepeth the sabbath from polluting it, and taketh hold of my covenant;*
>
> *Even them will I bring to my holy mountain, and make them joyful in my house of prayer: their burnt offerings and their sacrifices shall be accepted upon mine altar; for mine house shall be called an house of prayer for all people.*
>
> *The Lord GOD which gathereth the outcasts of Israel saith, Yet will I gather others to him, beside those that are gathered unto him.*
>
> ***Isaiah 56:1-8***

The period of history following the closing and sealing of truth in the Holy Scriptures was decreed by Yahwah, through the prophet Daniel. It specified that a period of changing of the Law, the seasons and blasphemy against the truth of Yahwah would follow the destruction of the holy temple and ancient Israelites. According to Daniel 7 this vision identifies the Catholic church and it's pontiff hierarchy as the source of this evil transgression.

> *Thus he said, The fourth beast shall be the fourth kingdom upon earth, which shall be diverse from all kingdoms, and shall devour the whole earth, and shall tread it down, and break it in pieces.*
>
> *And the ten horns out of this kingdom are ten kings that shall arise: and another shall rise after them; and he shall be diverse from the first, and he shall subdue three kings.*
>
> *And he shall speak great words against the most High, and shall wear out the saints of the most High, and think to change times and laws: and they shall be*

given into his hand until a time and times and the dividing of time.

But the judgment shall sit, and they shall take away his dominion, to consume and to destroy it unto the end.

And the kingdom and dominion, and the greatness of the kingdom under the whole heaven, shall be given to the people of the saints of the most High, whose kingdom is an everlasting kingdom, and all dominions shall serve and obey him.

Daniel 7:23-27

There is an admonishment in Thessalonians 5:21 to "Prove all things".

Prove all things; hold fast that which is good.

I Thessalonians 5:21

However, the New Testament and Christian teachings also contradicts itself on this point. How can one blindly "believe"? And, at the same time, seek to prove all things? The church hierarchy knows that whenever Christians begin to prove all things, especially where their own doctrine is concerned, they also know that the churches will become empty worship houses.

It is estimated that the four Gospels contain over a hundred references to the Hebrew Scriptures. These include Christ's own quotations from the scriptures as well as allusions to the Hebrew Scriptures. Among these are the following: "a man's enemies to be persons of his own household." Many people believe Jesus came to bring peace on earth. However this does not sound like "a Prince of Peace."

Think not that I am come to send peace on earth: I came not to send peace, but a sword.

For I am come to set a man at variance against his father, and the daughter against her mother, and the daughter-in-law against her mother-in-law.

And a man's foes shall be they of his own household.

Matthew 10:34-36

Compare this to the Old Testament Canon:

For the son dishonoreth the father, the daughter riseth up against her mother, the daughter-in-law against her mother-in-law; a man's enemies are the men of his own house.

Micah 7:6

This people draweth nigh unto me with their mouth, and honoreth me with their lips; but their heart is far from me.

But in vain they do worship me, teaching for doctrines the commandments of men.

Matthew 15:8-9

This precept has been forged and modified conveniently, to comply with Christian teachings. However, the precept quoted in Isaiah was originally based on an entirely different idea.

Wherefore the Lord said, Forasmuch as this people draw near me with their mouth, and with their lips do honor me, but have removed their heart far from me, and their fear toward me is taught by the precept of men:

Isaiah 29:13

The New Testament uses this Old Testament idea to suit its own purposes:

One witness shall not rise up against a man for any iniquity, or for any sin, in any sin that he sinneth: at the mouth of two witnesses, or at the mouth of three witnesses, shall the matter be established.

If a false witness rise up against any man to testify against him that which is wrong;

Then both the men, between whom the controversy is, shall stand before the Lord, before the priests and the judges, which shall be in those days;

And the judges shall make diligent inquisition: and, behold, if the witness be a false witness, and hath testified falsely against his brother;

Then shall ye do unto him, as he had thought to have done unto his brother: so shalt thou put the evil away from among you.

And those which remain shall hear, and fear, and shall henceforth commit no more any such evil among you.

And thine eye shall not pity; but life shall go for life, eye for eye, tooth for tooth, hand for hand, foot for foot.

Deuteronomy 19:15-21

It must be noted that the precept in Matthew is being used outside the context for which it was originally intended. People who read the Bible are familiar with certain terminology and phrases frequently spoken about in the Holy Scriptures. As a result, these phrases are cunningly used in the New Testament to snare the unsuspected reader.

But if he will not hear thee, then take with thee one or two more, that in the mouth of two or three witnesses every word may be established.

Matthew 18:16

Another example of a false interpretation involves the one Scriptural injunction against killing versus another injunction against murder.

> *Ye have heard that it was said by them of old time, Thou shalt not kill; and whosoever shall kill shall be in anger of the judgment*
>
> ***Mathew 5:21***

Compared to Exodus 20:13 states: " *Thou shalt not murder"* has a different connotation. Israelites were permitted to kill when justified. For example, in self-defense or even in some cases, as punishment to violators of the Law. Interestingly enough is how the book of Matthew modifies the Hebrew prophecies to fit Jesus thereby creating the promised Messiah concept. The modifications created by Christendom is unacceptable to both Israelites past and present. It is of particular concern to Israel for whom the accounts were originally intended. The aforementioned prophecies and precepts are clear examples of gross distortions of truth as applied to Jesus in Christian doctrine. These distorted prophecies include:

> *And I said unto them, If ye think good, give me my price; and if not, forbear. So they weighed for my price thirty pieces of silver.*
>
> *And the Lord said unto me, Cast it unto the potter: a goodly price that I was prised at of them. <u>And I took the thirty pieces of silver,</u> and cast them to the potter in the house of the Lord.*
>
> ***Zechariah 11:12-13***

It is important to note that originally Zechariah gives a figure of thirty pieces of silver in a transaction which had nothing to do with the passages quoted in Jeremiah and Matthew. The precept in Jeremiah 32:6-10, explains how Jeremiah purchased a field as a sign that the captivity of Israel would return. In this passage we read that he paid seventeen shekels of silver. In Matthew 27:7-10, which contradicts its own statement concerning the quote in Jeremiah.

Then Judas, which had betrayed him, when he saw that he was condemned, repented himself, and brought again the thirty pieces of silver to the chief priests and elders,

Saying, I have sinned in that I have betrayed the innocent blood. And they said, What is that to us? see thou to that.

And he cast down the pieces of silver in the temple, and departed, and went and hanged himself.

And the chief priests took the silver pieces, and said, It is not lawful for to put them into the treasury, because it is the price of blood.

And they took counsel, and bought with them the potter's field, to bury strangers in.

Wherefore that field was called, The field of blood, unto this day.

Then was fulfilled that which was spoken by Jeremiah the prophet, saying, And they took the thirty pieces of silver, the price of him that was valued, whom they of the children of Israel did value;

And gave them for the potter's field, as the Lord appointed me.

Matthew 27:3-9

Under close scrutiny it is quite obvious, that the precept recorded in Matthew has been stolen, is inaccurately quoted and is clearly taken out of context. The price mentioned in Jeremiah quoted below indicates that seventeen shekels of silver was paid for the field. More importantly it had nothing to do with an event which took place some 600 years later.

And Jeremiah said, The word of the Lord came unto me, saying,

> *Behold, Hanameel the son of Shallum thine uncle shall come unto thee, saying, Buy thee my field that is in Anathoth: for the right of redemption is thine to buy it.*
>
> *So Hanameel mine uncle's son came to me in the court of the prison according to the word of the Lord, and said unto me, Buy my field, I pray thee, that is in Anathoth, which is in the country of Benjamin: for the right of inheritance is thine, and the redemption is thine; buy it for thyself. Then I knew that this was the word of the Lord.*
>
> *And I bought the field of Hanameel my uncle's son, that was in Anathoth, and weighed him the money, even seventeen shekels of silver.*
>
> *And I subscribed the evidence, and sealed it, and took witnesses, and weighed him the money in the balances.*
>
> ***Jeremiah 32:6-10***

Each of these precepts has been cleverly manipulated to create the Jesus myth. The original context in which these ideas were presented had nothing to do with Jesus or Christianity. No degree of belief can change this fact. It is important to recognize the framework as well as the purpose for all the so-called Gospels.

The second Gospel was supposedly written by Mark. Some scholars identify John Mark as the writer, while other scholars conclude that it is virtually impossible to determine which Mark actually wrote this Gospel. Regardless of the fact that scholars cannot agree upon whether Mark, Marcus, or Marcanas actually wrote that particular Gospel, they do agree that the book was written by someone who was not an eye-witness to the events. There is insufficient evidence to substantiate whether any of these alleged persons ever lived or knew Jesus. Tradition indicates that Mark's Gospel was provided by Peter's information rather than his own personal experience. The time and place scholars believe Mark's Gospel was first made public was in Rome approximately 70 CE. Although Mark appears to have written primarily for the Romans, this record also contains many quotations from and references to the Hebrew Scriptures.

Under close examination there is a clearly calculated and deliberate pattern used throughout each book in the Greek writings to use quotations from and references to the Hebrew Scriptures as a means of validation for their reports.

In the Gospel of Luke there is also basis for uncertainty about the accuracy of his account of the events. Unsurprisingly, all of the events recorded in the Gospels rely squarely on its own sources within the Greek writings as supportive evidence. Little or no evidence exist elsewhere about the historical accounts of the period which can validate New Testament allegations.

The very purpose of the Gospel is to provide accounts of the ministry of Jesus Christ. Strangely enough, the very documents which attempt to relate the historical record to us under carefully scrutiny becomes questionable about its own accuracy and truthfulness. The significant questions which emerge concerning the validity and truthfulness within the Greek writings is entirely uncharacteristic of the Hebrew Scriptures.

In some instances, the alleged writers of the Gospel were not attributed to Matthew, Mark, Luke or John until the second century CE a period as much as 150 years after the death of Jesus and nearly a century after any of the alleged writers themselves. The Gospel's authenticity is allegedly based on numerous Hebrew scriptural references. They also contain quotations which are inserted without proper context because the Hebrew Scriptures are made within a different context. This is indicative of the method and pattern used by the anonymous scribes of the Greek writings to create a harmony between the New Testament and the Hebrew Scriptures. The particular purpose for the formation of the bible is that the fusion of the two books become a means by which to eliminate the original true Book of God.

The "good news" or "Gospel" according to John is another one of the four versions allegedly recorded of Jesus Christ's early life. The accounts of John's Gospel represents the last Gospel written about the alleged ministry of Jesus. The Gospel books of Luke and John do not name the writers. As early as the second century, the authorship of the books was rejected on the grounds that some groups considered the book's teaching unorthodox. The advent of modern "critical" scholarship has also challenged John's authorship.

The following examples represent specific cases of how Christian doctrine has deliberately changed Truth into falsehood. However, the commentaries here makes a plain discourse about what is real and unreal.

> *And it came to pass in the days of Ahaz the son of Jotham, the son of Uzziah, king of Judah, that Rezin the king of Syria, and Pekah the son of Remaliah, king of Israel, went up toward Jerusalem to war against it, but could not prevail against it.*
>
> *And it was told the house of David, saying, Syria is confederate with Ephraim. And his heart was moved, and the heart of his people, as the trees of the wood are moved with the wind.*
>
> *Then said the Lord unto Isaiah, Go forth now to meet Ahaz, thou, and Shear-jashub thy son, at the end of the conduit of the upper pool in the highway of the fuller's field;*
>
> *And say unto him, Take heed, and be quiet; fear not, neither be fainthearted for the two tails of these smoking firebrands, for the fierce anger of Rezin with Syria, and of the son of Remaliah.*
>
> *Because Syria, Ephraim, and the son of Remaliah, have taken evil counsel against thee, saying,*
>
> *Let us go up against Judah, and vex it, and let us make a breach therein for us, and set a king in the*

midst of it, even the son of Tabeel:

Thus saith the Lord God, It shall not stand, neither shall it come to pass.

For the head of Syria is Damascus, and the head of Damascus is Rezin; and within threescore and five years shall Ephraim be broken, that it be not a people.

And the head of Ephraim is Samaria, and the head of Samaria is Remaliah's son. If ye will not believe, surely ye shall not be established.

Moreover the Lord spoke again unto Ahaz, saying,

Ask thee a sign of the Lord thy God; ask it either in the depth, or in the height above.

But Ahaz said, I will not ask, neither will I tempt the Lord. And he said, Hear ye now, O house of David; Is it a small thing for you to weary men, but will ye weary my God also?

Therefore the Lord himself shall give you a sign; Behold, a virgin shall conceive, and bear a son, and shall call his name Immanuel.

Butter and honey shall he eat, that he may know to refuse the evil, and choose the good.

For before the child shall know to refuse the evil, and choose the good, the land that thou abhorrest shall be forsaken of both her kings.

Isaiah 7:1-16

The historical setting described in this passage of Isaiah occurred approximately 740 years before the purported birth of Jesus. It is impossible to understand this passage without the proper understanding of the context of the historical period to which the message is directed. Christian doctrine has created their own interpretation of the seventh chapter and fourteenth verse which purports that the child to be called Emmanuel is a prediction of the birth of Jesus. The facts will reveal there is nothing further from the Truth. The evidence which sheds light on this issue begins in the first verse of the seventh Chapter. Whenever the details support the main idea or theme in a passage it helps to prove the meaning and establish the facts.

Here are the details which prove that it is impossible to link this message of the Prophet Isaiah to Jesus or Christian doctrine. At least seven centuries prior to the Christian era there lived a king of Judah in northeast Africa in the land of Israel whose name was Ahaz. Ahaz was the son of Jotham and the grandson of Uzziah who were also kings of Judah. In the days of King Ahaz of Judah a conflict arose when Resin. Resin the king also known as King of Syria joined forces with Remaliah, king over Israel and the Northern Kingdom, joined themselves to wage war against the southern kingdom of Judah. The national split between Judah and Ephraim under the leadership of Jeroboam the son of Nebat escalated into a potential civil war. As a result, the northern tribes of Israel formed a confederacy with the external forces of Syria against their brother Judah who represented the dynasty of king David.

The overwhelming forces of the united armies of Syria and the ten northern tribes became a source of tremendous concern and fear for king Ahaz and the people of Judah. In verse 3, YAHWAH instructs the Prophet Isaiah to go forth to meet Ahaz with his son Shear-Yashub in the end of the fullers field.

Shear-Yashub, the son of Isaiah, was so named by Yahwah as a sign and reminder to Isaiah that a remnant of Israel would return from the predicted future captivity. The English translation of Shear-Yashub is "a remnant shall return." The Most High Yah's message by Isaiah to Ahaz, was not to worry or fear but trust in YAH and do not regard the bragging, empty threats, and anger of Rezin, Kind of Syria. In verses 5-6, the Prophet discloses the plot and identifies the parties behind the political conspiracy. Their unjust challenge to the throne of Judah and house of David is denounced. First Kings 11-30 says, "And Ahijah laid hold of the garment that was on him and rent it in twelve pieces. And he said to

Jeroboam: "take thee ten pieces for thus saith Yahwah, the God, the Power of Israel: Behold, I will rend the kingdom out of the hand of Solomon and will give ten tribes to thee but he shall have one tribe for my servant David's sake and for Jerusalem's sake, the city which I have chosen out of all the tribes of Israel."

The proper understanding of this historical background is an excellent example of the numerous facts which undermine the Christian attempt to link Jesus with this period in the Old Testament. The sequence of events continues to unfold with the statement recorded in verse 5 of Isaiah, chapter7, which says, "because Aram hath counseled evil against thee, Ephraim also, and the son of Remaliah, saying, "let us go up against Judah and vex it and let us make a breach therein for us, and set up a king in the midst of it, even the son of Tabeel."

The motives behind this conspiracy of evil to unite against Judah also became an act against the will of the God of Israel. By their unjust replacement of Ahaz Yahwah's opposition is clearly stated. In verse 7, the Prophet reiterates the message of YAHWAH to Ahaz, "Thus saith YAHWAH: it shall not stand, neither shall it come to pass. Verse 8-9 provides additional evidence about the specific time frame in which the Most High would destroy these enemies confronting Judah and dissolve the pressures of subjugation and their fears of oppression with in 65 years.

Clearly at this point in the passage recorded in the 7th chapter of Isaiah there is not a remote connection between this episode in history and anything associated with Christianity. The facts taken in context as we continue will show that there is no way anyone can conclude logically or otherwise prove that verse 14 in itself points to the birth of Jesus.

Looking back in the book of Isaiah, Chapter7, Verse 10: "And the Lord Yahwah spoke again to Ahaz saying, Ask thee a sign of the Lord Yahwah thy God: Ask whether in the depth, or in the height above." Here Ahaz is commanded to ask for a sign. He may ask for it in heaven or he can ask for assign in the earth. On the contrary, in verse 12, Ahaz responds by saying, "But Ahaz said, I will not ask neither will I try the Lord." The Prophet's disapproval of His response is the reason for an even more vehement determination to shorten the time span of the judgment against the combined forces of Syria and the northern kingdom of Israel. “And he said, hear ye now, O house of David, Is it a small thing for you to weary men, that ye will weary my God also?”

In verse 13, Isaiah expresses how Ahaz’s disobedience has been a source of personal weariness and trouble for the people in general. He further admonishes the king for not complying with the command to ask Yahwah for a sign. King Ahaz’s hesitance is seen as a source of weariness to Yahwah because he was told to ask for a sign and he refused to do so. The verses 7:14-16 reinforce and support the argument that there is absolutely no connection or link to Jesus or Christian doctrine.

“Therefore, the Lord Yahwah Himself shall give you a sign: Behold the young woman shall conceive, and bear a son, and shall call his name Emmanuel.” Here the prophet declares that Yahwah Himself will provide a sign to symbolize the certainty of all words spoken by Isaiah in the name of Yahwah to King Ahaz..

In many Bibles a bad translation has distorted the meaning of this verse. The key here is the incorrect use of the English word “virgin.” he Hebrew word in the original text is עלמה (Al’mah) which means a young woman. The word בתולה (B’Tulah) is the Hebrew word for virgin and is not present in this verse. However, it has become the primary translation used in the Kings James Version. The birth of a son, at the time of prophecy, took place. He was symbolic as the name Emmanuel was to be a sign for Ahaz, the king of the people of Judah. Emmanuel translated means “God is with us.” This was the confidence and necessary faith in Yahwah by Ahaz the king needed at this time of great peril. The following verses make it clear that the time projected to resolve this issue is directly tied with the birth of a child which was named Emmanuel at that time.

Verse 15 indicates the element of time represented by the metaphor “curd and honey, shall he eat, when he knoweth to refuse the evil an choose the good. Yea before the child shall know to refuse the evil, and choose the good, the land whose two kings thou hast a horror of shall be forsaken." These words were indicative of the fact that Yahwah would destroy the enemies of the king before the childhood of Emmanuel came to an end.

The facts and other points presented in these verses are in support of the theme or main idea that King Ahaz has been instructed not to fear these two opposing forces of Syria and Israel. Isaiah's intervention is to strengthen Ahaz, King of Judah and solicit his faith in the message brought to him in the name of Yahwah.

The birth of the child Emmanuel was a sign for that particular time. The early childhood characteristics marked a diminish from 65 years to a much shorter time described by the time it takes a child to reach an age where he is capable of eating curd and honey or the age where he will know how to refuse evil and choose good. In other words, even before the child could discern between good and evil would those nations be destroyed as well as their vain threats.

Isaiah states:

For a child is born unto us, A son is given unto us,And the government is upon his shoulder; and his Name is called:

פלא יועץ אל גבור אבי עד שר שלום

For unto us a child is born, unto us a son is given: and the government shall be upon his shoulder: and his name shall be called Wonderful, Counselor, The mighty God, The everlasting Father, The Prince of Peace.

The government may be increased, and of peace, there be no end, upon the throne of David, and upon his kingdom, to establish it, and to uphold it through justice and through righteousness from henceforth even for ever the zeal of the YAH of HOSTS doth perform this.

Isaiah 9:5-6

Once again the time associated with the historic period is during the lifetime of the Prophet Isaiah which was approximately 700 years prior to the supposed birth of Jesus. From a grammatical standpoint in the Hebrew language nothing could be clearer to indicate that this precept has no connection with Jesus or Christian teachings. If the precept quoted above in Isaiah 9:6 referred to the birth of Jesus it would be stated in Hebrew in the future tense and translated accordingly. However, in Hebrew and in the English translation, it points to the past tense. Isaiah understood that in these events the birth of the child mentioned had already taken place. Note that it says for a child is born unto us (past tense), a son is given unto us (also past tense), and the government is upon his (present tense) shoulder and his name is called wonder in counsel is God the mighty, the everlasting Father, Prince of Peace.

Properly understood, the reference is to Hezekiah the son of Ahaz in whose days Isaiah prophesied. Isaiah's statements does not pertain to the future. He is not saying a son will be born or a son will be given but rather is already given unto us because Hezekiah was the Crowned Prince who was recognized from his youth to be the righteous successor to the throne of his father King Ahaz. The government rested upon his shoulder because his righteous character gave hope to the immediate future of the Kingdom of Judah. Thus, the government is upon his shoulders. The Prince of Peace identified the title of Crowned Prince, the son of the king who was designated to be king. Hezekiah grew up as a peaceful youth designated to ascend to the throne of his father Ahaz.

In honor and praise of the Creator who alone establishes any king is the exaltation, "wonderful in counsel is God the mighty, the everlasting Father," translated from Isaiah 9:6. Imagine nearly a thousand years later Christian interpreters of the Holy Scriptures concluding that Isaiah 9:5 and an untold number of other Hebrew scriptures referred to Jesus. Isaiah 9:5, describes certain attributes of the Creator, Yah, and has nothing to do with the so-called Christian Savior, Jesus Christ. How Inappropriate. However, consider the manipulations and modifications used in Christian doctrine and the manner in which they use the phrase, "prince of peace" which was ascribed to Hezekiah in verse 5. The title is taken from this precept, modified in concept and wrongfully attributed to Jesus. This is another case of high-handed deception. Isaiah 9:6 clearly confirms the commentary presented for it says that "the government may be increased or continued, and of peace there be no end, upon the throne of David, and upon his kingdom, to establish it, and to uphold it through justice and through righteousness. From henceforth and forever, the zeal of the Lord, Yahwah, of hosts doeth perform this."

Isaiah Chapter 9:6 also strengthens the point because it shows that the Prophet speaks about the particular government and throne associated with the lineage and realm of King David's descendants, his sons who were to rule over the nation of Israel. Isaiah's declaration is that Yahwah will establish it and uphold it through acts of justice and righteousness manifested during the reign of Hezekiah and even forever.

The messiah issue has also become a newly created idea based upon the practice of anointed kings promised to reign on the throne of David forever.

> *And there shall come forth a rod out of the stem of Jesse, and a Branch shall grow out of his roots: 2 And the spirit of Yawah shall rest upon him, the spirit of wisdom and understanding, the spirit of counsel and might, the spirit of knowledge and of the fear of YAHWAH;*
>
> ***Isaiah 11:1-2***

The aforementioned precepts refers to a descendant of king David who was the chosen son of Jesse, anointed as king of Israel from whose roots a son will be established with the restoration of God, Yahwah's scattered people. The conspirators of Christian doctrine would be remiss if they failed to take advantage of the opportunity to use these precepts as a reference to Jesus. Let's face it, metaphors like "a shoot" shall come forth, out of the stock of Jesse and twig shall grow forth out of his roots provide the greatest or as good and opportunity as any of the other seemingly ambiguous precepts to which Jesus has been forced into place as its reference. Moreover, in light of Biblical investigation. This is where and how Christian teachers have created the "Myth of the Messiah."

Can the Greek writings refute the authority of the Holy Scriptures? Absolutely not. The Old Testament is the authority on the facts and Truth in the Bible. The facts in the Old Testament fundamentally refute all modifications in the New Testament on the subject of Israelite history.

Half-truths, falsehoods and blatant lies which have been woven into a shrewdly manipulated fabrication in the New Testament have been a major source of deception for millions of Bible readers. The Christian religion itself is a snare, which has trapped and imprisoned millions of souls. It is impossible to know the Truth in the Bible and at the same time embrace Christianity. Christianity is a contradiction to the Truth. Historical evidence also reveals that the great controversy based upon opposing views about ideas concerning Christian doctrine has always existed within Christian circles alone. Today, the gap is wider than ever.

The restoration of Truth is simply an idea whose time has come. Again, as according to prophecy, the return of the Nation of Israel will occur simultaneously with the return of the Truth. This viewpoint represented in the Hebrew Scriptures is nowhere to be found in Christian doctrine. In fact it is completely and overtly contradicted in the Greek writings. Why?

In lieu of the tremendous number of discrepancies between the Hebrew Scriptures/Israelite teachings and Greek writings/Christian teachings it is in incumbent upon every sincere seeker of Truth to exercise the greatest discernment in reading the Bible.

There is absolutely no middle ground between Hebrew Scriptures and Greek writing. Neither is there any way to adhere to Israelite Law and accept Christian doctrine at the same time. In other words, it is impossible to comply with instructions to obey God's law and Christian teachings, which annuls His law. In similar fashion it is inconceivable to acknowledge GOD as the Eternal Invisible Creator and a mortal man who died approximately at 33 years of age.

PLAGIARISMS IN THE NEW TESTAMENT

Plagiarisms in the New Testament are inserted in the text throughout the Greek scriptures in order to give credibility to its authorship. Under proper examination it becomes obvious that these excerpts from the Hebrew scriptures (Old Testament) which have been inserted into Greek scriptures (New Testament) do not fit into the historical context of the period. In many instances the statements and/or names are misspelled, quoted inaccurately, moreover these quotations are misrepresented in the New Testament text.

OLD TESTAMENT (ORIGINAL)	NEW TESTAMENT (MODIFIED)
Isaiah 7:14 Therefore the Lord Himself shall give you a sign: behold, the young woman shall conceive and bear a son and shall call his name Immanuel.	**Matthew 1:22-23** So all this was done that it might be fuffilled which was spoken by the Lord through the prophet, saying. "Behold, the virgin shall bewith child, and bear a son and they shall call his name Immanuel' which is translated, "God with us"
Micah5:1 But thou. Beth-lehem Ephrathah. which are Little to be among the thousands of Judah, Out of thee shall one come forth unto me That is to be ruler in Israel; Whose going Forth are from of old, from ancient days.	**Matthew 2:6** 'But you, Bethlehem, in the land of Judah, are not the least among the rulers of Judah; for out of you shall come a ruler who will shepherd my people Israel.'

Hosea 11:1
When Israel was a child, then I loved him And out of Egypt I called my son.

Matthew 2:15
And was there until the death of Herod, that it might be fulfilled which was spoken by the Lord through the prophet, saying, "out of Egypt I called my son"

Jeremiah 31:15
Thus saith the Lord; a voice is heard in Ramah, lamentation and bitter weeping, Rachel weeping for her children, she refuseth to be comforted for her children, because they are not.

Matthew 2:18
"And a voice was heard in Ramab, lamentation, weeping, and great mourning Rachel weeping for her children, refusing to be comforted, because they were no more."

Daniel 2:44
And in the days of those kings shall the God Of heaven set up a kingdom, which shall Never be destroyed; nor shall the kingdom be left to another people. It shall break in pieces and consume all these kingdoms, but it shall stand forever.

Matthew 3:2
And saying, "Repent, for the kingdom of heaven is at hand!"

Isaiah 40:3
Hark! One calleth: Clear ye in the wilderness the way of the Lord, Make plain in the desert a highway for our God.

Matthew 3:3
For this is he who was spoken of by the prophet Isaiah, saying: "The voice of one crying in the wilderness. 'Prepare the way of the Lord; make His path straight'

II Kings 1:8
And they answered him: 'He was a hairy man, And girt with a girdle of leather about his loins.' and he said. 'It is Elijah the Tishbite.'

Matthew 3:4
Now John himself was clothed in camel's hair with a leatherbelt around hiswaist and his food was locust and wild honey.

Deuteronomy 8:3
And He afflicted thee, and suffered thee to hunger, And fed thee with manna, which thou knewest not Neither did thy fathers know: that He might make thee know that man doth not live by bread only, But by every thing that procedeth out of the mouth Of the Lord doth man live.

Matthew 4:4
But He answered and said "It is written, 'Man shall not live by bread alone, but by every word that proceeds from the mouth of God.'"

Psalm 91:11
For He will give His angels charge over thee to keep thee in all thy ways. They shall bear thee upon their hands lest thou dash thy foot against a stone.

Matthew 4:6
And said to Him, 'If You are the son of God, throw yourself down. For it is written:

'He shall give His angels charge over you,' and, 'In their hands they shall bear you up, lest you dash your foot against a stone."'

Deuteronomy 6:16
Ye shall not try the Lord your God, as ye Tried Him in Massah

Matthew 4:7
Jesus said to **him,** 'It is written again. 'You shall not tempt the Lord your God"'

Deuteronomy 6:13
Thou shalt fear the Lord thy God: And Him shall thou serve, and by His name thou Shall swear.

Matthew 4:10
Then Jesus said to him, "Away with you, Satan! For it is written, 'You shall worship the Lord your God, and Him only you shall serve'"

Isaiah 9:1-2
The people that walked in darkness Have Seen a great light; they that dwelt in the Land of the shadow of death, upon them Hath the light shined. Thou hast multiplied the nation, thou hast increased their joy; they before thee according to the joy and harvest, as men rejoice when they divide the spoil.

Matthew 4:15-16
The land of Zebulun and the land of Naphtali, by the way of the sea, beyond the Jordan, Galilee of the Gentiles: The people who sat in darkness have seen a great light, and upon those who sat in the region and shadow of death light has dawned."

Isaiah 61:2
To proclaim the year of the Lord's good Pleasure, and the day of vengeance of our God; to comfort all that mourn.

Matthew 5:4
Blessed are those who mourn, for they shall be comforted.

Psalm 37:11
But the meek shall inherit the earth, and they shall delight themselves in abundant peace.

Matthew 5:5
Blessed are the meek, for they shall inherit the earth.

Isaiah 55:1-2
Ho, everyone that thirsteth, come ye for water, And he that hath no money; come ye, buy, and eat; Yea, come, buy wine and milk without money. And without price. Wherefore do ye

Matthew 5:6
Blessed are those who hunger and thirst for righteousness, for they shall be filled.

spend money for that which is not bread? And your gain for that which satisfieth not? Hearken diligently unto me, and eat ye that which is good, And let your soul delight itself in fatness.

Psalm 24:4-5
He that hath clean hands, and a pure heart, Who hath not taken My name in vain, and hath not sworn deceitfully. He shall receive a blessing from the Lord and righteousness from the God of his salvation.

Matthew 5:8
Bleesed are the pure in heart, for they shall see God.

Exodus 20:13
Thou shalt not murder. (kill)

Deuteronomy 5:17
Thou shalt not murder. (kill)

Matthew 5:21
"Ye have heard that it was said by them of old time, Thou shalt not kill; and whosoever shall kill shall be in danger of the judgment:"

DISCREPANCIES IN DEATH & RESURRECTION OF JESUS

Let us be clear. If there was no birth of Jesus. There was no resurrection. Neither was there any immaculate conception. Matthew, Mark, Luke, John each tell of the burial, death and resurrection of Jesus. However, their accounts differ greatly and therefore have caused scholars to have many suspicions as to their veracity. There are obvious contradictions about who they say was present at the time and many misgivings concerning what happened. In lieu of the tremendous number of discrepancies, between the Old and New Testament, and in the New Testament itself, it is incumbent upon every sincere seeker of truth to exercise the greatest care and discernment in reading the Bible.

> *Consider the point made in these precepts concerning resurrection before you examine the chart.*
>
> *Is there not an appointed time to man upon earth? are not his days also like the days of an hireling?*
>
> *As a servant earnestly desireth the shadow, and as an hireling looketh for the reward of his work:*
>
> *So am I made to possess months of vanity, and wearisome nights are appointed to me.*
>
> *When I lie down, I say, When shall I arise, and the night be gone? and I am full of tossings to and fro unto the dawning of the day.*
>
> *My flesh is clothed with worms and clods of dust; my skin is broken, and become loathsome.*
>
> *My days are swifter than a weaver's shuttle, and are spent without hope.*
>
> *O remember that my life is wind: mine eye shall no more see good.*

The eye of him that hath seen me shall see me no more: thine eyes are upon me, and I am not.

As the cloud is consumed and vanisheth away: so he that goeth down to the grave shall come up no more.

He shall return no more to his house, neither shall his place know him any more.

Job 7:1-10

For there is hope of a tree, if it be cut down, that it will sprout again, and that the tender branch thereof will not cease.

Though the root thereof wax old in the earth, and the stock thereof die in the ground;

Yet through the scent of water it will bud, and bring forth boughs like a plant.

But man dieth, and wasteth away: yea, man giveth up the ghost, and where is he?

As the waters fail from the sea, and the flood decayeth and drieth up:

So man lieth down, and riseth not: till the heavens be no more, they shall not awake, nor be raised out of their sleep.

Job 14:7-12

According to the Holy Scriptures and in accordance with life's experiences no one has ever or will ever get out of a grave and returned unto the Creator.

In total contradiction to the truth the First Epistle Of Paul to the Thessalonians writes the following in Chapter 4:13-18.

But I would not have you to be ignorant, brethren, concerning them which are asleep, that ye sorrow not, even as others which have no hope.

For if we believe that Jesus died and rose again, even so them also which sleep in Jesus will God bring with him.

For this we say unto you by the word of the Lord, that we which are alive and remain unto the coming of the Lord shall not prevent them which are asleep.

For the Lord himself shall descend from heaven with a shout, with the voice of the archangel, and with the trump of God: and the dead in Christ shall rise first:

Then we which are alive and remain shall be caught up together with them in the clouds, to meet the Lord in the air: and so shall we ever be with the Lord.

Wherefore comfort one another with these words.

This chart below is an illustration, which highlights this example. The discrepancies have been underlined for your convenience.

Burial

Matthew 27:57-66

57 When the even was come, there came a
rich man of Arimathaea, named Joseph, who
also himself was Jesus' disciple: 58 He went to
Pilate, and begged the body of Jesus. Then
Pilate commanded the body to be delivered. 59
And when Joseph had taken the body, he
wrapped it in a clean linen cloth, 60 And laid it
in his own new tomb, which he had hewn out
in the rock: and he rolled a great stone to the
door of the sepulcher, and departed. 61 And
there was Mary Magdalene, and the other
Mary, sitting over against the sepulcher. 62
Now the next day, that followed the day of the
preparation, the chief priests and Pharisees
came together unto Pilate, 63 Saying, Sir, we

remember that that deceiver said, while he was yet alive, After three days I will rise again. 64 Command therefore that the sepulcher be made sure until the third day, lest his disciples come by night, and steal him away, and say unto the people, He is risen from the dead: so the last error shall be worse than the first. 65 Pilate said unto them, Ye have a watch: go your way, make it as sure as ye can. 66 So they went, and made the sepulcher sure, sealing the stone, and setting a watch.

Mark 15:42-47

42 And now when the even was come, because it was the preparation, that is, the day before the sabbath, 43 Joseph of Arimathaea, an honorable counselor, which also waited for the kingdom of God, came, and went in boldly unto Pilate, and craved the body of Jesus. 44 And Pilate marveled if he were already dead: and calling unto him the centurion, he asked him whether he had been any while dead. 45 And when he knew it of the centurion, he gave the body to Joseph.46 And he bought fine linen, and took him down, and wrapped him in the linen, and laid him in a sepulcher which was hewn out of a rock, and rolled a stone unto the door of the sepulcher. the mother of Jesus beheld where he was laid.

Luke 23:50-56

50 And, behold, there was a man named Joseph, a counselor; and he was a good man, and a just: 51 (The same had not consented to the counsel and deed of them;) he was of Arimathaea, a city of the Jews: who also himself waited for the kingdom of God.52 This man went unto Pilate, and begged the body of Jesus. 53 And he took it down, and wrapped it

in linen, and laid it in a sepulcher that was hewn in stone, wherein never man before was laid. 54 And that day was the preparation, and the sabbath drew on. 55 And the women also, which came with him from Galilee, followed after, and beheld the sepulcher, and how his body was laid. 56 And they returned, and prepared spices and ointments; and rested the sabbath day according to the commandment.

John 19:38-42

38 And after this Joseph of Arimathaea, being a disciple of Jesus, but secretly for fear of the Jews, besought Pilate that he might take away the body of Jesus: and Pilate gave him leave. He came therefore, and took the body of Jesus. 39 And there came also Nicodemus, which at the first came to Jesus by night, and brought a mixture of myrrh and aloes, about a hundred pound weight. 40 Then took they the body of Jesus, and wound it in linen clothes with the spices, as the manner of the Jews is to bury. 41 Now in the place where he was crucified there was a garden; and in the garden a new sepulcher, wherein was never man yet laid. 42 There laid they Jesus there-fore because of the Jews' preparation day; for the sepulcher was nigh at hand.

The Resurrection

Matthew 28:1-15

In the end of the sabbath, as it began to dawn toward the first day of the week, came Mary Magdalene and the other Mary to see the sepulcher. 2 And, behold, there was a great earthquake: for the angel of the Lord de-scended from heaven, and came and rolled back the stone from the door, and sat upon it. 3

His countenance was like lightning, and his raiment white as snow: 4 And for fear of him the keepers did shake, and became as dead men. 5 And the angel answered and said unto the women, Fear not ye: for I know that ye seek Jesus, which was crucified. 6 He is not here: for he is risen, as he said. Come, see the place where the Lord lay. 7 And go quickly, and tell his disciples that he is risen from the dead; and, behold, he goeth before you into Galilee; there shall ye see him: lo, I have told you. 8 And they departed quickly from the sepulcher with fear and great joy; and did run to bring his disciples word. 9 And as they went to tell his disciples, behold, Jesus met them, saying, All hail. And they came and held him by the feet, and worshiped him. 10 Then said Jesus unto them, Be not afraid: go tell my brethren that they go into Galilee, and there shall they see me. 11 Now when they were going, behold, some of the watch came into the city, and showed unto the chief priests all the things that were done. 12 And when they were assembled with the elders, and had taken counsel, they gave large money unto the soldiers,13 Saying, Say ye, His disciples came by night, and stole him away while we slept. 14 And if this come to the governor's ears, we will persuade him, and secure you. 15 So they took the money, and did as they were taught: and this saying is commonly reported among the Jews until this day.

Mark 16:1-11

And when the sabbath was past, Mary Magdalene, and Mary the mother of James, and Salome, had bought sweet spices, that they might come and anoint him. 2 And very early

in the morning the first day of the week, they
came unto the sepulcher at the rising of the
sun. 3 And they said among themselves, Who
shall roll us away the stone from the door of
the sepulcher? 4 And when they looked, they
saw that the stone was rolled away: for it was
very great. 5 And entering into the sepulcher,
they saw a young man sitting on the right side,
clothed in a long white garment; and they were
affrighted. 6 And he saith unto them, Be not
affrighted: Ye seek Jesus of Nazareth, which
was crucified: he is risen; he is not here:
behold the place where they laid him. 7 But go
your way, tell his disciples and Peter that he
goeth before you into Galilee: there shall ye
see him, as he said unto you. 8 And they went
out quickly, and fled from the sepulcher; for
they trembled and were amazed: neither said
they any thing to any man; for they were
afraid. 9 Now when Jesus was risen early the
first day of the week, he appeared first to
Mary Magdalene, out of whom he had cast
seven devils.10 And she went and told them
that had been with him, as they mourned and
wept. 11 And they, when they had heard that
he was alive, and had been seen of her,
believed not.

Luke 24:1-12

Now upon the first day of the week, very early
in the morning, they came unto the sepulcher,
bringing the spices which they had prepared,
and certain others with them. 2 And they found
the stone rolled away from the sepulcher. 3
And they entered in, and found not the body of
the Lord Jesus. 4 And it came to pass, as they
were much perplexed thereabout, behold, two
men stood by them in shining garments: 5 And

as they were afraid, and bowed down their
faces to the earth, they said unto them, Why
seek ye the living among the dead? 6 He is not
here, but is risen: remember how he spake
unto you when he was yet in Galilee, 7 Saying,
the Son of man must be delivered into the
hands of sinful men, and be crucified, and the
third day rise again. 8 And they remembered
his words,
9 And returned from the sepulcher, and told all
these things unto the eleven, and to all the rest.
10 It was Mary Magdalene and Joanna, and
Mary the mother of James, and other women
that were with them, which told these things
unto the apostles. 11 And their words seemed
to them as idle tales, and they believed them
not. 12 Then arose Peter, and ran unto the
sepulcher; and stooping down, he beheld the
linen clothes laid by themselves, and departed,
wondering in himself at that which was come
to pass.

John 20:1-18

The first day of the week cometh Mary
Magdalene early, when it was yet dark, unto
the sepulcher, and seeth the stone taken away
from the sepulcher. 2 Then she runneth, and
cometh to Simon Peter, and to the other
disciple, whom Jesus loved, and saith unto
them, They have taken away the Lord out of
the sepulcher, and we know not where they
have laid him. 3 Peter therefore went forth,
and that other disciple, and came to the
sepulcher. 4 So they ran both together: and the
other disciple did outrun Peter and came first
to the sepulcher. 5 And he stooping down, and
looking in, saw the linen clothes lying; yet went
he not in. 6 Then cometh Simon Peter follow-

ing him, and went into the sepulcher, and seeth the linen clothes lie,7 And the napkin, that was about his head, not lying with the linen clothes, but wrapped together in a place by itself. 8 Then went in also that other disciple, which came first to the sepulcher, and he saw, and believed. 9 For as yet they knew not the Scripture, that he must rise again from the dead. 10 Then the disciples went away again unto their own home. 11 But Mary stood without at the sepulcher weeping: and as she wept, she stooped down, and looked into the sepulcher, 12 And seeth two angels in white sitting, the one at the head, and the other at the feet, where the body of Jesus had lain. 13 And they say unto her, Woman, why weepest thou? She saith unto them, Because they have taken away my Lord, and I know not where they have laid him.14 And when she had thus said, she turned herself back, and saw Jesus standing, and knew not that it was Jesus. 15 Jesus saith unto her, Woman, why weepest thou? whom seekest thou? She, supposing him to be the gardener, saith unto him, Sir, if thou have borne him hence, tell me where thou hast laid him, and I will take him away. 16 Jesus saith unto her, Mary. She turned herself, and saith unto him, Rabboni; which is to say, Master. 17 Jesus saith unto her, Touch me not; for I am not yet ascended to my Father: but go to my brethren, and say unto them, I ascend unto my Father, and your Father; and to my God, and your God. 18 Mary Magdalene came and told the disciples that she had seen the Lord, and that he had spoken these things unto her.

KING DAVID AND THE MESSIAH ISSUE

And it shall come to pass, when thy days be expired that thou must go to be with thy fathers, that I will raise up thy seed after thee, which shall be of thy sons; and I will establish his kingdom.

He shall build me an house, and I will stablish his throne for ever.

I will be his father, and he shall be my son: and I will not take my mercy away from him, as I took it from him that was before thee:

But I will settle him in mine house and in my kingdom for ever: and his throne shall be established for evermore.

According to all these words, and according to all this vision, so did Nathan speak unto David.

1st Chronicles 17:11-15

European Jews were the first religion to develop the idea of "The Messiah. The concept was modified from writings in the Holy Scriptures which pertained to King David and the restoration of his future generations upon his throne with the return of Israel in the end of days. The idea rose out of a need to provide hope for Jews in the face of severe persecutions which they experienced among, Greeks, Romans and in latter times throughout Western and Eastern Europe. In fact, the Spanish inquisition initiated a pattern of victimization and expulsion of Jews in countries from one end of Europe to the other.

Many Jewish Martyrs experienced harsh deaths in some of the most gruesome ways one could imagine. These pious Jews choose to die for their religion, rather than abandon their beliefs or make conversion. Although Jews were eventually able to acquire a homeland in Palestine, this came after hundreds of years of cruel suffering in Germany, Poland, Hungary and Russia. Nevertheless, their hope for the coming of the messiah never ceased. Their establishment of the state of Israel in 1948 has not brought peace to them or on earth as they believe would occur when the messiah comes.

The late Rabbi Menachem Mendel Schneerson, the former head of the Chabad-Lubavitch Movement who last resided in the Crown Heights section of Brooklyn, New York was recognized by many Jewish Sects as the Messiah. His death astonished and crushed the hopes of thousands of Jews who failed to see their prophetic vision accomplished during their lifetime. Even after his death many Jews still believe he will rise from his grave located in Springfield Gardens in Queens, New York, where a vigilant watch is kept. At the time of his death in June 12, 1994 many Jews invaded the area to purchase homes.

The following quotes from Jews, God and History by Max I. Dimont described clearly what prompted the Jewish creation of a messiah.

> "For two centuries goverment by Judges worked, but the system had one fatal weakness. It did not provide the basis for a strong centralized leadership. Each Judge was selected by his own tribe. In times of crisis, the tribes were convinced, God would unite them and send an "inspired leader" who, like Joan of Arc, would deliver them from evil. So firm were they in this conviction that no sucessor was ever provided. Each crisis, they felt, would itself create a Deliverer. In this "Deliverer" we see the roots of the messianic concepts to come."

> "A new hope was sweeping the ranks of the Jews. A military messiah had arisen among them. A great scholar was his apostle and armor-bearer. The messiah on horseback was Simon ben Cozeba, or bar Kochba ("Son of the Star"),and the scholar was Rabbi Akiba. This combination of an armored messiah and revered rabbi was the catalytic agent that coalesced the dispirited Jews into a new fighting force."

> "It was Rabbi Akiba who confirmed Simon bar Kochba's claim that he was a messiah and a descendant of King David. When the two issued a call to arms against the Romans, Jews of every sect by the tens of thousands flocked to the standards, but not the Christians, who were caught in a dilemma. The Christians were suffering as much as the Jews, if not more, under the Roman yoke and would under normal circumstances have joined the Jews in rebellion. But, already having a messiah in Jesus, they could not accept another messiah in bar Kochba, and thus they could not join the Jews in the showdown with the Romans."

In similar fashion , the idea of the Christian Messiah emerged as a result of the massive slaughters and great carnage in the arenas in Rome and throughout the Western World at the start of the common era. At the time of the fall of the Roman Empire many poor people chose Christianity as a religion because they believed all souls who accepted Jesus Christ and his message would enter heaven. The advent or second coming of Christ became the source upon which Christianity was able to create its own concept of a Messiah in Jesus Christ.

> "The essene Jews developed a messianic religion, giving birth to the ideas which were to play a dominant role in the lives of John the Baptist and Jesus."

> "Jesus Christ is Greek for 'Joshua the messiah' the word 'messiah' comes from the Hebrew word mashiah, meaning 'one who is anointed,' that is a messiah."

> "He was a oasis of comfort in a desert of Roman misery. The humble people flocked to him to take solace in his words, to find comfort in his vision, and to take heart in the hope he held out."

However, the Holy Scriptures or Old Testament firmly established the point that the "Anointed" Monarch lineage through King David will be restored with the gathering and restoration of the Nation of Israel.

There is literally no mention of the coming of a Messiah anywhere in the Old Testament. The concept which has been driven by Jews and/or Christians from the either the word "Masheahk" "Anointed" or Masheah "Savior" does not exist in the original Hebrew thought or writings.

The concept of a Messiah is a foreign idea which first began among the founders of Judaism. Jewish scholars or rabbis were the first to interpret aspects of Israelite prophecies as the coming of the Messiah. Similarly in later times Christian founders reinterpreted the Holy Scriptures to suit their Christian doctrine. Thus, they identifed the coming of Jesus Christ, as the coming of the Messiah. It is crucial to understand exactly who Jews are, in respect to bible history. Jews are generally European converts, creators of a a set of beliefs that would later be called Judaism. In the Old Testament the word "Jew" does not exist. On the other hand, Israelites are descendants of the original ancient Hebrew Israelites. In no way are Jews and Israelites synonymous.

> "Jews, Jewish and Judaism, represents the religion established by the European couterparts of Israel or Yisrael. It may be shocking, but neither of these three terms are represented or found in the Hebrew language, nor can they be directly translated into Hebrew. The word Israel or Yisrael, represents a nation and not a religion.
>
> Alfred Lilenthal, a prominant member of the Jewish Community expressed this thought on January 6, 1975, in a midwest magazine stating. "Many of the Europeans were converted to the Jewish faith in places far from Palestine and therefore, were not native to the Holy Land.
>
> George Friendman in his book, The End of the Jewish People pointedly states "The Europeans who are claiming to be Jews, are nothing more than Hebrew speaking gentiles."
>
> *Israelites And Jews The Significant Difference*
> *Cohane Michael*

It is important to understand that the word יהודה "Yehudah" is correctly translated "Judah" in English. However, it has been erroneously mistranslated as the word "Jew", by Jewish scholars. Judah was the last tribe to be conquered among Israel. King David's house, a family of the tribe of Judah, was established as the royal family. They were appointed the anointed kings in the Nation of Israel to reign forever. The kings of Israel were anointed kings of the Creator. They were literally anointed with oil and in a more spiritual sense, this meant they were divinely appointed by the Most High. The Hebrew word for anointed is משח "MaSheahk" in Hebrew. The English word "messiah" is derived from the Hebrew משעה "MaSheah", which means "savior". The two words sound similar in pronounciation in the Hebrew language, but they have distinct and different meanings. The rabbis who founded Judaism or the Jewish religion started the concept of the Messiah. In later times Christian founders patterned their Messiah concept after the so-called Jews. A modified version replaced the original Hebrew meaning. Consequently, nowadays we hear about the Jew's messiah and the Christian messiah, respectively. Ironically, both have lived and died, while the prophecies in the Holy Scriptures, remain void and unfulfilled.

The anointed or Ha MaSheahk, has been substituted by Christians for the Hebrew "MaSheah." However, the word MaSheahk is applicable solely to a future son, a descendant of King David who will return as king with the restoration of Yahwah's chosen people. The word "savior" has been substituted for "anointed" in some translations because, it helps to camouflage the truth, and support their teachings that Jesus is the Savior. In this instance, the facts can only be known by those who read Hebrew. Therefore, the ability to investigate on this level requires knowledge of the Hebrew language.

Daniel 9:25 and verse 26 contain precepts sited erroneously by Christian teachers as proof that Jesus is God and the savior of the world. However, if a correct translation and intellectual reasoning is presented instead of deception, then their beliefs present quite a different picture.

> *Know therefore and understand, that from the going forth of the commandment to restore and to build Jerusalem unto the Messiah the Prince shall be seven*

weeks, and threescore and two weeks: the street shall be built again, and the wall, even in troublous times.

And after threescore and two weeks shall Anointed Messiah be cut off, but not for himself: and the people of the prince that shall come shall destroy the city and the sanctuary; and the end thereof shall be with a flood, and unto the end of the war desolations are determined.

Daniel 9:25-26

Correctly translated it should read:

Know therefore and understand, that from the going forth of the commandment to restore and to build Jerusalem unto the Anointed Prince shall be seven weeks, and threescore and two weeks: the street shall be built again, and the wall, even in troublous times.

And after threescore and two weeks shall the Anointed cut off, but not for himself: and the people of the prince that shall come shall destroy the city and the sanctuary; and the end thereof shall be with a flood, and unto the end of the war desolations are determined.

Daniel 9:25-26

Again, in Isaiah 45:1 the Hebrew word "MaSheahk" is translated accurately as "anointed" and again it does not apply to Jesus as part of Christian doctrine. However, because the precept in Daniel is referred to and used by Christians the word "MaSheahk" is wrongfully translated to mean "savior". This can only be a deliberate error.

Thus saith the Lord to his anointed, to Cyrus, whose right hand I have holden, to subdue nations before him; and I will loose the loins of kings, to open be-

fore him the two leaved gates; and the gates shall not be shut;

Isaiah 45:1

When we look in Matthew 16:13-16, and 22:41-46, it is plain to see that the point made by Matthew is in conflict with the statement made in Mark. There is an attempt to substitute Jesus as the recipient of the promise made to King David. However, the passage in Matthew tells us that there is no certainty as to who Jesus the son of man is. The true identity of Jesus is questioned in several places of the New Testament. It is a question that has never been answered.

When Jesus came into the coasts of Caesarea Philippi, he asked his disciples, saying, Whom do men say that I the Son of man am?

And they said, Some say that thou art John the Baptist: some, Elijah; and others, Jeremiah, or one of the prophets.

He saith unto them, But whom say ye that I am?

And Simon Peter answered and said, Thou art the Christ, the Son of the living God.

Matthew 16:13-16

While the Pharisees were gathered together, Jesus asked them,

Saying, What think ye of Christ? whose son is he? They say unto him, The son of David.

He saith unto them, How then doth David in spirit call him Lord, saying,

The Lord said unto my Lord, Sit thou on my right hand, till I make thine enemies thy footstool?

If David then call him, Lord, how is he his son?

And no man was able to answer him a word, neither durst any man from that day forth ask him any more questions.

Matthew 22:41-46

Matthew 22:44-45 was taken from Psalms 110:1. Once again, this is a case of Christian teachers attempting to force Jesus into the Holy Scriptures and force their false beliefs on the world.

The scepter shall not depart from Judah, nor a lawgiver from between his feet, until Shiloh come; and unto him shall the gathering of the people be.

The 49th chapter of Genesis are Jacob's last words to his twelve sons before his death. It is a message directed strictly to each of his children. In fact, his address to them begins with Rueben his firstborn and continues in order of their birth down to his youngest son Benjamin. Verse 10, Jacob provides for Judah his fourth son his Yah-inspired vision of Judah's future in the hearing of his other brothers. Jacob's Divine prophetic vision befell each of the 12 tribes of Israel in later times.

In Judah's particular case he is told that Judah would become the perpetual leader among the twelve tribes. This was fulfilled when the Creator established and chose king David of the tribe of Judah as the anointed king of Israel. David's house or seed was made king in Israel forever. (Chronicles 22:6-10), (Kings 8:15-20)

Then he called for Solomon his son, and charged him to build a house for the Lord God of Israel.

And David said to Solomon, My son, as for me, it was in my mind to build a house unto the name of the Lord my God:

But the word of the Lord came to me, saying, Thou hast shed blood abundantly, and hast made great wars: thou shalt not build a house unto my name, because thou hast shed much blood upon the earth in my sight.

Behold, a son shall be born to thee, who shall be a man of rest; and I will give him rest from all his enemies round about: for his name shall be Solomon, and I will give peace and quietness unto Israel in his days.

He shall build a house for my name; and he shall be my son, and I will be his father; and I will establish the throne of his kingdom over Israel forever.

I Chronicles 22:6-10

And he said, Blessed be the Lord God of Israel, which spoke with his mouth unto David my father, and hath with his hand fulfilled it, saying,

Since the day that I brought forth my people Israel out of Egypt, I chose no city out of all the tribes of Israel to build a house, that my name might be therein; but I chose David to be over my people Israel.

And it was in the heart of David my father to build a house for the name of the Lord God of Israel.

And the Lord said unto David my father, Whereas it was in thine heart to build a house unto my name, thou didst well that it was in thine heart.

Nevertheless thou shalt not build the house; but thy son that shall come forth out of thy loins, he shall build the house unto my name.

And the Lord hath performed his word that he spoke, and I am risen up in the room of David my father, and sit on the throne of Israel, as the Lord promised, and have built a house for the name of the Lord God of Israel.

I Kings 8:15-20

"As long as men come to Shiloh or until Shiloh come" merely meant with the exception of the time the prophet Ahijah from Shiloh who appeared to Jeroboam to state that he would be given ten tribes and Judah two tribes to keep a lamp as promised by Yahwah. Judah would forever be ruler in Israel. The precept recorded in Genesis 49:10 has baffled both Christian and non-Christian. Many Bible teachers and scholars also have been unable to explain or understand this verse.

> *And it shall come to pass, if thou shalt hearken diligently unto the voice of the Lord thy God, to observe and to do all his commandments which I command thee this day, that the Lord thy God will set thee on high above all nations of the earth:*
>
> *And all these blessings shall come on thee, and overtake thee, if thou shalt hearken unto the voice of the Lord thy God.*

The blessings were short lived due to disobedience to the law. As a consequence, the following curses overtook the people and ultimately the nation and their kings were taken as captives and became slaves among the nations of the world.

> *But it shall come to pass, if thou wilt not hearken unto the voice of the Lord thy God, to observe to do all his commandments and his statutes which I command thee this day; that all these curses shall come upon thee, and overtake thee:*
>
> *Cursed shalt thou be in the city, and cursed shalt thou be in the field.*
>
> *Cursed shall be thy basket and thy store.*
>
> *Cursed shall be the fruit of thy body, and the fruit of thy land, the increase of thy kine, and the flocks of thy sheep.*
>
> *Cursed shalt thou be when thou comest in, and cursed shalt thou be when thou goest out.*

The Lord shall send upon thee cursing, vexation, and rebuke, in all that thou settest thine hand unto for to do, until thou be destroyed, and until thou perish quickly; because of the wickedness of thy doings, whereby thou hast forsaken me.

Deuteronomy 28:15-20

The precept below help explain what happened, why it happened and where it happened. Because they rejected the law of Yah, Israel and their king were taken into captivity among the nations and forced to worship false gods.

Thy sons and thy daughters shall be given unto another people, and thine eyes shall look, and fail with longing for them all the day long: and there shall be no might in thine hand.

The fruit of thy land, and all thy labors, shall a nation which thou knowest not eat up; and thou shalt be only oppressed and crushed always:

So that thou shalt be mad for the sight of thine eyes which thou shalt see.

The Lord shall smite thee in the knees, and in the legs, with a sore botch that cannot be healed, from the sole of thy foot unto the top of thy head.

The Lord shall bring thee, and thy king which thou shalt set over thee, unto a nation which neither thou nor thy fathers have known; and there shalt thou serve other Gods, wood and stone.

And thou shalt become an astonishment, a proverb, and a byword, among all nations whither the Lord shall lead thee.

Deuteronomy 28:32-37

> *Thou shalt beget sons and daughters, but thou shalt not enjoy them; for they shall go into captivity.*
>
> ***Deuteronomy 28:41***

There is a conglomeration of evidence to show that the prophets denounced and admonished Israel's rejection of Yah's Law. The Holy Scriptures repeatedly speak of Yah's righteous indignation because of His people's rebellion.

The Davidic line of Kings have been identified among modern nations of our present time. For example in Uganda their tradition has maintained a record of thirty-one dynasties tracing back to the lineage of King David. However, the most recognized and renown descendant has been recorded in the Ethiopian Annuals known as the Kebra Nagast which links King Solomon and Mekeda, Queen of Sheba, who gave birth to the King's son Menelik 1. The name Menelik literally means from the king. Meen=From Melek=King, thus, from the King. The late Emperor Haile Selassie was acknowledged during his lifetime as the most royal blooded monarch on earth tracing back to Solomon. First Kings 14:7-8. He bore the title "Conquering Lion of Judah," even though he reigned on the throne in Ethiopia.

Contrary to Christian teachings the prophets in the holy Scriptures, say a King shall reign and prosper, and shall execute judgment and justice in the earth from the branch of David.

> *Behold the days come, saith the Lord, that I will raise unto David a righteous Branch, and a King shall reign and prosper, and shall execute judgement and justice in the earth.*
>
> *In his days Judah shall be saved, and Israel shall dwell safely: and this is his name whereby he shall be called, YAHWAH OUR RIGHTEOUSNESS.*
>
> *Therefore, behold, the days come, saith the Lord, that they shall no more say, The Lord liveth, which brought up the children of Israel out of the land of Egypt;*

But, The Lord liveth, which brought up and which led the seed of the house of Israel out of the north country, and from all countries whither I had driven them; and they shall dwell in their own land.

Jeremiah 23:5-8

In Verse 7, the controversy surrounding the issue of whether or not the fulfillment of prophecy will follow the path according to the Old Testament or New Testament will undeniably settle the issue of Davidic King or Christian Messiah Jesus.

In Christian doctrine there is absolutely no connection in the literal sense between the aforementioned prophesy of Jeremiah 23:7-8, and Jesus Christ. The specific reference of the prophecy in the chapter points to a time when Yahwah will raise up from the scattered people of Israel a descendant from the seed of David, who will possess a righteous nature. The son of David will be established as King of Judah and Israel in the Holy Land.

This occurrence will also usher in prosperity, salvation and safety in the midst of the restored nation. This is completely different from any Christian expectation or doctrine concerning the future.

See now that I, even I, am he, and there is no God with me: I kill, and I make alive; I wound, and I heal: neither is there any that can deliver out of my hand.

Deuteronomy 32:39

No one has the power to intervene against the Almighty to deliver anyone from His decree. Yahwah alone has the power to give life, take it away, afflict punishment and restore health and healing.

If we stretch our imagination and attribute Jesus to a descendant of King David, then that would mean he was an Israelite? Ancient Israelites are African by geographical and physical characteristics. The Hebrew Scriptures is of an eastern rather than western origin. On the contrary, the Greek Scriptures is of a western origin. And they pointedly portray Jesus as being of European descent.

Behold, the days come, saith the LORD, that I will perform that good thing which I have promised unto the house of Israel and to the house of Judah.

In those days, and at that time, will I cause the Branch of righteousness to grow up unto David; and he shall execute judgment and righteousness in the land.

In those days shall Judah be saved, and Jerusalem shall dwell safely: and this [is the name] wherewith she shall be called, The LORD our righteousness.

For thus saith the LORD; David shall never want a man to sit upon the throne of the house of Israel;

Neither shall the priests the Levites want a man before me to offer burnt offerings, and to kindle meat offerings, and to do sacrifice continually.

And the word of the LORD came unto Jeremiah, saying,

Thus saith the LORD; If ye can break my covenant of the day, and my covenant of the night, and that there should not be day and night in their season;

[Then] may also my covenant be broken with David my servant, that he should not have a son to reign upon his throne; and with the Levites the priests, my ministers.

As the host of heaven cannot be numbered, neither the sand of the sea measured: so will I multiply the seed of David my servant, and the Levites that minister unto me.

Moreover the word of the LORD came to Jeremiah, saying,

Considerest thou not what this people have spoken, saying, The two families which the LORD hath chosen, he hath even cast them off? thus they have despised my people, that they should be no more a nation before them.

Thus saith the LORD; If my covenant [be] not with day and night, [and if] I have not appointed the ordinances of heaven and earth;

Then will I cast away the seed of Jacob, and David my servant, [so] that I will not take [any] of his seed [to be] rulers over the seed of Abraham, Isaac, and Jacob: for I will cause their captivity to return, and have mercy on them.

Jeremiah 33:14-26

Finally, it is in these precepts, we see the Almighty Yah has made it emphatically clear that the House of David shall rule over Judah and Israel. They shall not depart, nor the Levites cease to be priests before Him. This clearly points to the fact that the concept of the coming of the Messiah, is a foreign idea that exists nowhere in the Holy Scriptures. The literal understanding is that the restoration of the people of Israel, would take place in conjunction with the restoration of the lineage from King David. When one accurately reads the scriptures in the proper sequential order, with the proper understanding of the historical/prophetic context, no other conclusion can be derived.

And David the king came and sat before the LORD, and said, Who am I, O LORD God, and what is mine house, that thou hast brought me hitherto?

And yet this was a small thing in thine eyes, O God; for thou hast also spoken of thy servant's house for a great while to come, and hast regarded me according to the estate of a man of high degree, O LORD God.

What can David speak more to thee for the honour of thy servant? for thou knowest thy servant.

O LORD, for thy servant's sake, and according to thine own heart, hast thou done all this greatness, in making known all these great things.

O LORD, there is none like thee, neither is there any God beside thee, according to all that we have heard with our ears.

And what one nation in the earth is like thy people Israel, whom God went to redeem to be his own people, to make thee a name of greatness and terribleness, by driving out nations from before thy people, whom thou hast redeemed out of Egypt?

For thy people Israel didst thou make thine own people for ever; and thou, LORD, becamest their God.

Therefore now, LORD, let the thing that thou hast spoken concerning thy servant and concerning his house be established for ever, and do as thou hast said.

Let it even be established, that thy name may be magnified for ever, saying, The LORD of hosts is the God of Israel, even a God to Israel: and let the house of David thy servant be established before thee.

For thou, O my God, hast told thy servant that thou wilt build him an house: therefore thy servant hath found in his heart to pray before thee.

And now, LORD, thou art God, and hast promised this goodness unto thy servant:

Now therefore let it please thee to bless the house of thy servant, that it may be before thee for ever: for thou blessest, O LORD, and it shall be blessed for ever.

1st Chronicles 17:16-27

And there shall come forth a rod out of the stem of Jesse, and a Branch shall grow out of his roots:

And the spirit of the LORD shall rest upon him, the spirit of wisdom and understanding, the spirit of counsel and might, the spirit of knowledge and of the fear of the LORD;

And shall make him of quick understanding in the fear of the LORD: and he shall not judge after the sight of his eyes, neither reprove after the hearing of his ears:

But with righteousness shall he judge the poor, and reprove with equity for the meek of the earth: and he shall smite the earth with the rod of his mouth, and with the breath of his lips shall he slay the wicked.

And righteousness shall be the girdle of his loins, and faithfulness the girdle of his reins.

Isaiah 11:1-5

CONCLUSION

And it shall come to pass in the last days, that the mountain of the Lord's house shall be established in the top of the mountains, and shall be exalted above the hills; and all nations shall flow unto it.

And many people shall go and say, Come ye, and let us go up to the mountain of the LORD, to the house of the God of Jacob; and he will teach us of his ways, and we will walk in his paths: for out of Zion shall go forth the law, and the word of the LORD from Jerusalem.

Isaiah 2:2-3

When the Bible is disassembled properly its allows people to see how original concepts in the Old Testament that have been misrepresented in the New Testament. The true meaning of the Bible has become a hidden treasure within its pages to be found only by those determined to know the truth. The canonization of the Bible and construction of the New Testament has created patterns of deception, distortion, contradictions and confusion for those who thought the Bible to be the source and message of common heritage. It is undeniable when the facts are known that the Old Testament and New Testament are based upon the teaching of two different ethnic groups with two different sets of concepts and two entirely different deities.

When we look at the scriptures, in order to understand them in their fullness, as a book of history and prophecy we see the unique and ageless story of the Nation of Israel. They are a "peculiar" holy people unto the Lord their God: and He has chosen them to be a special people unto Himself, above all people that are upon the face of the earth.

For thou art an holy people unto the LORD thy God,

> *and the LORD hath chosen thee to be a peculiar people unto himself, above all the nations that are upon the earth.*
>
> ***Deuteronomy 14:2***

If the Bible is viewed as a source of information from a single, authority with instructions from one God then under these circumstances, the Bible will never be properly understood.

If a Bible reader is unaware of who exactly the true nation of Israel is, the correct comprehension of biblical history will not be fully understood. If a Bible reader has no knowledge of the original languages used in the Bible, then there is absolutely no way to compare or recognize changes or mistranslation.

In any reading passage, clues are provided within paragraphs, before paragraphs and after the particular paragraph in which a comprehensive question arises. When reading the Bible there is no exception. This reading skill must always be applied rather than abandoned. The redemption of Israel by Yahwah who proclaimed their captivity as well as their redemption from Babylon is in no way connected or associated with Jesus or the period in which he supposedly lived.

Understanding the sum of the historical facts from Genesis to Chronicles in the Old Testament easily establishes that there is no connection with the New Testament or Christian doctrine. The plot in the Old Testament deals with how the Creator of heaven and earth called Abraham from Ur of Chaldee and promised to give him the land of Cannan. The Creator also promised to make him the father of a multitude of nations. Abraham is told that through his seed shall all the nations of the earth be blessed on earth. There is indisputable evidence, which proves that billions of people throughout the world trace their roots to Abraham. Abram was a descendant of Noah's son Shem, the father of Shemitic people.

East Indians, West Indians, Indians, Pakistanis, Afghanistans, Ishmaelites, Iraqis, Iranians, Ebos, Ashanti, Falashas, Zulu, Syrians, Saudi

Arabians, are some of the better known Shemites. Blacks or African Israelites in the Diaspora are practically unknown Shemites. The Bible distinguishes itself from many other books in that the truth within its pages is established with indisputable evidence on the earth. In fact, the genealogy is represented in earth exactly according to the accounts recorded in Genesis. A history of a people and their genealogy cannot be assimilated into a religion based on a belief system.

There are twelve (12) families or tribes which comprise ancient Israelites who were the sons of Jacob and whose name was changed to Israel. Jacob and Esau were fraternal twins born to Isaac and Rebekah. Abraham was the father of a multitude of nations. The covenanted seed of Abraham are his descendants through the lineage of Isaac and Jacob. Subsequently, the Creator identifies himself as the God of Abraham, Isaac and Jacob, or, the "God of Israel." The primary focus of the Bible concerns itself with Israel as the chosen people of Yahwah. The entire message in the Old Testament or Holy Scriptures deals with Yahwah's involvement with His controversial chosen people.

Israel's disobedience, rebellion, stiffneckedness, and rejection of God's Laws and His Prophets form the plot within the pages of the Old Testament or Holy Scriptures. The resolution to the plot and the fulfillment of the prophecies is described as a return to God and obedience to His laws. The literal gathering of the Nation of Israel is the true testimony of these facts, which can't be ignored, in any earnest Bible scholarship.

Bible study has been a basic form of education for ages. In fact, among prominent universities such as Yale and Harvard, the study of the Hebrew language, history and culture still remains an area of study that garners the highest esteem. An intelligent approach to Bible study is to engage the subject matters in its books with the use of the most basic critical thinking and reading skills, i.e., reading, thinking and reasoning. Knowing means getting the facts together. In order to know, an investigation of the literature must entail understanding, applying knowledge, analyzing, synthesizing and evaluating. Knowing the Bible requires the ability to classify information.

For example, it is necessary to recognize and understand the classification of the various genealogies. There must be a clear distinction between the real and the fanciful. Definitions due to translations must be precise. Fact and opinion must be plainly identifiable. Understanding of the Bible literature is achieved through proper comparing and contrasting of information. Especially, due to the opposing ideas recorded in the Hebrew Scriptures or Old Testament, and the Greek writings or New Testament. It is important to recognize the structures represented in the presentations of the respective original languages of Hebrew and Greek and there translations into the English language. Truth consists of many clues, which leads to facts.

Structure must include identifying the time and place of the event or history. It is essential to identify the characters in the history. The various plots must be seen in sequence of events from beginning to the climax right through to the Bible's truthful ending. Another important key to knowing the Truth about and within the bible is the ability to establish the proper sequence in the correct order in which things occurred in the Bible. Figurative language is used throughout the Bible, metaphors, parables, and other figurative language must be correctly interpreted. Comparisons of word meanings are also an effective tool used in intelligent Bible study. Identifying the main ideas and relationships of individuals throughout the Bible is crucial. For example, the subject, pronouns, such as I, you, he, she, it, they, we, and our, must be accurately related to the subjects to which the pronoun refers. To infer means to look at the evidence and come to a conclusion based on that evidence. That is, you look at the facts and you infer the answer. Inference skills are pivotal to reading and understanding the Bible. At times, study of the Bible requires an ability to form an idea or conclusion on very little evidence. However, the use of conjecture is based upon the logical use of the facts given rather than wild unsupported speculations.

Many of the problems encountered in reading and studying the Bible can be solved only if you have all the necessary information. In the analyzing process, judgment must be based on completeness. Therefore, one needs to read thoroughly and gather all the necessary information you would need before you make judgment or draw a conclusion. To solve a problem, Bible scholars and students must be like reporters. A reporter must give exact and complete information. Accurate analyzation will be enhanced tremendously, if the bible student or reader is able to distinguish abstract meaning from the concrete meaning.

For example, some words are more general than others . For instance, the word man is more general than the word Adam, because man refers to a whole group of people and Adam refers to one person. Critical to the thinking process towards analyzing the Bible is the skill to recognize logic and action as well as the historical logic. The hypothesis that the Truth is to be separated from the lies in the Bible has to be inclusive of historical logic and logic of actions. If a statement is logical, it makes sense. Again, paramount to this process of analyzing is the ability to recognize the fallacies.

A very significant difference observed about the Hebrew Scriptures or Old Testament and the Greek writings or New Testament is that the history in the Hebrew Scriptures begins in Genesis and unfolds in a chronological manner with verifiable dates and supportive details until the closing period of the written record. On the contrary, the alleged history in the Greek writings begins in four different books with several variations of the accounts. Beyond Matthew, Mark, Luke and John some writings within the Greek canonization, the New Testament, are not really books, but personal letters which are not YAHWAH'S inspired messages. The Hebrew Scriptures existed long before any Greek writings came into existence. The Hebrew Scriptures was the regarded Holy writings allegedly studied and recognized by Jesus, the Apostles, Disciples and everyone associated with that time period. The Hebrew Scriptures has been the only recorded inspired word of Yahwah in the world for thousands of years.

The phrase, "Thus saith the Yahwah" appears nowhere in the entire Greek writing or New Testament. There is no concrete evidence to confirm that any of the miracles described in the Greek writings ever took place. On the contrary, the accounts of the Creator recorded by Moses unmistakably happened and became a God-inspired writing. The flood as well as the lives of Noah and his sons, Shem, Ham and Japeth are all proven to have been true events.

Abraham, his descendants, and their existence within geographical locations have been verified. The enslavement of Israel in Egypt is validated by relics and annuls of neighboring societies at the time. Their deliverance from Egypt and occupation of Canaan land has been substantiated.

On the question of genealogy, the Hebrew Scriptures accounts of genealogies are all verifiable and reflect accurately among the inhabitants worldwide. Aaron, Joshua, Samuel, David, Solomon, etc.. However, The genealogy of the Greek writings are inaccurate and unverifiable.

The chronology of the history recorded in the Holy Scriptures/Old Testament is also the basis upon which the Hebrew calendar is formed. As a result, the history and calendar originate from the same source and therefore, are one and the same. The source of history of the Hebrew Scriptures is verified in the historical time periods of the Hebrew calendar and the calendar is synchronized with the history. As Truth upholds itself the Hebrew Scriptures corroborates itself with and through historical facts substantiated by an accurate time line or calendar. This is not the case with the Greek writings or New Testament.

An honest analysis of the Bible could not possibly ignore or dismiss the need to research into the history, culture and languages of the people and societies recorded in the scripture, and in what is termed "secular history." When we view the course of man's journey through time, we see the unfolding of all of Yah's prophecies, which we understand, will culminate with the restoration of the Nation of Israel, the restoration of King David's Throne the Kingdom of Yah and the Levitical Priesthood. History, does not occur outside of the realm of the Bible or the Plan of Yah. They are one, and the same.

All Christian theory or doctrine is predicated on the belief that Jesus existed. The fact that there is absolutely no concrete proof that Jesus existence is nothing more than a belief. Beliefs can come and go at a whim, factual history, of which the Old Testament Scriptures are the highest example of will always stand. The word of the Lord, the true Yah of Creation is the everlasting standard. Some Christians have said that the Old Testament concealed is the New Testament revealed to suggest that what is hidden in the Old Testament (concerning Jesus) is revealed inthe New Testament. This simply is a false statement.

> *But the Lord is the true God, he is the living God, and an everlasting king: at his wrath the earth shall tremble, and the nations shall not be able to abide his indignation.*
>
> *Thus shall ye say unto them, The gods that have not made the heavens and the earth, even they shall perish from the earth, and from under these heavens.*
>
> *He hath made the earth by his power, he hath established the world by his wisdom, and hath stretched out the heavens by his discretion.*
>
> ***Jeremiah 10:10-12***
>
> *For the earth shall be filled with the knowledge of the glory of the LORD, as the waters cover the sea.*
>
> ***Habakkuk 2:14***
>
> *And Yahwah shall be king over all the earth: in that day shall there be one Yahwah, and his name one.*
>
> ***Zechariah 14:9***

PROPHET CHRONOLOGY

Each prophet in the Holy Scriptures prophesied in the days and during the reign of one or more kings in Israel. A prophet may have prophesied before the rulers and people in the Northern Kingdom or Southern Kingdom. The names of the particular kings before which each prophet brought the word of Yah is recorded in the 1st chapter of the each prophet's book. Presented below is a chart which displays the Kings, prophets and time of prophecies

CHAPTER	KINGS	TIME OF PROPHECY (BC)
Isaiah 1:1	The vision of Isaiah the sons of Amos which he saw concerning Judah and Jerusalem in the days of Uzziah, Jotham, Ahaz and Hezekiah kings of Judah.	765-696
Jeremiah 1:1	The words of Jeremiah the son of Hilkiah of the Priest that were in Anathoth in the land of Benjamin to whom the word of the Lord came in the days of Judah, in the thirteenth year of his reign. It came also in the days of Jehoiakim the son of Josiah, king of Judah, unto the carrying away of Jerusalem captive in the fifth month.	628-585
Ezekiel 1:1	Now it came to pass in the thirtieth year, in the fourth month, in the fifth day of the month, as I was among the	595-536

	captives by the river Chebar, that the heavens were opened, and I saw visions of G-d. In the fifth year of king Jehoiachin's captivity the word of the Lord came expressly unto Ezekiel the priest, the son of Buzi, in the land of the Chaldonns by the river Chebar: and the hand of the Lord was there upon him.	
Hosea 1:1	The word of the Lord that came unto Hosea the son of Beeri, in the days of Uzziah, Jotham, Ahaz, and Hezekiah kings of Judah, and in the days of Jeroboam the son of Joash, king of Israel.	800-725
Joel 1:1	The word of the Lord that came to Joel the son of Pethuel.	810-795
Amos 1:1	The words of Amos, who was among the herdmen, of Tekoa, which he saw concerning Israel in the days of Uzziah king of Judah and in the days of Jereboam the son Joash King of Israel, two years before the earthquake.	810-785
Obadiah 1:1	The vision of Obadiah: Thus saith the Lord God concerning Edom.	588-583

Jonah 1:1	Now the word of the Lord came unto Jonah the son of Ammitai.	810-784
Micah 1:1	The word of the Lord that came to Micah the Morashite in the days of Jotham, Ahaz, and Hezekiah, kings of Judah, which he saw concerning Samaria and Jerusalem.	758-699
Nahum 1:1	The burden of Nineveh, the book of the vision of Nahum the Elkoshite.	728-698
Habakkuk 1:1	The burden which Habakkuk the prophet did see.	612-598
Zephaniah 1:1	The word of the Lord which came unto Zephaniah the son of Cushi, the son of Gedaliah, the son of Amariah, the son of Hezekiah in the days of Josiah the son of Amon king of Judah.	640-609
Haggai 1:1	In the second year of Darius the king, in the sixth month, in the first day of the month came the word of the Lord by Haggai the prophet unto Zerubbael the son of Shealtiel, governor of Judah, and to Joshua the son of Jehozadak, the	539-518

	High Priest, saying: Thus speaketh the Lord of Hosts.	
Zechariah 1:1	In the eight month, in the second year of Darius, came the word of the Lord unto Zechariah the son of Berechiah the son of Iddo the prophet saying:	539-510
Malachi 1:1	The burden of the word of Lord of Israel by Malachi.	436-397
Daniel 1:1	In the third year of the reign of Jehoiakim king of Judah came Nebuchadnezzar king of Babylon unto Jerusalem and besieged it.	606-534
Ezra 1:1	Now in the first year of Cyrus King of Persia, that the word of Lord by the mouth Jeremiah might be accomplished.	536-516
Nehemiah 1:1	The words of Nehemiah the son of Hacaliah. Now it came to pass in the twentieth year, as I was in Shushan the castle.	464-424

Levitical Communications Inc
P.O Box 1324
Bear. DE. 19701

Phone/Fax (302) 834 5375

Websites:
www.hebrewisraelites.com
www.leviticalcommunication.com

BIBLIOGRAPHY

American Heritage Dictionary, Houghton, Mufflin & Co., Boston, 1985

Ammi, Ben, God, The Black Man & Truth, Washington, DC, Communicators Press, 1991

Armstrong, Herbert, W., The United States and Briton in Prophecy, Worldwide Church of God, 1980

Chomsky, William, Hebrew The Eternal Language, Philadelphia, The Jewish

Dimont, Max I. - Jews, God and History Publication Society of America, 1958

Glenn, Menahem G., PhD, Hamillon Hamassi Practical Hebrew-English Dictionary, New York, Hebrew Publishing Company, 1947

Good News / New Testament, Today's English Version, American Bible Society, 1976

Guyana Chronicle, Minister Asserts the Bible is Hoax, Guyana, Sunday, February 22, 1987

Holy Bible Containing the Old and New Testament (The), Reference Edition, Aprocrypha King James Version, New York, American Bible Society, 1971

Holy Scriptures (The), The Jewish Publication Society of America, Philadelphia, 1955

Josephus, Flavius, Life & Works of Josephus - Antiquities of the Jews, Philadelphia, Toronto, John C. Winston Company, 1957

Levine, Samuel, You Take Jesus, I'll Take God, Los Angeles, Hamorah Press, 1980

New York Daily News, Christmas, New York, Sunday, December 23, 1979

New York Daily News, Shroud of Turin Has Human DNA, New York, Sunday, March 29, 1998

Smith's Bible Dictionary, Philadelphia, A.J. Holmon Company

World Book Encyclopedia, World Book Inc., Field Enterprises Educational Corporation, USA, 1965

Williams, Joseph, J., Hebrewism of West Africa, New York, Biblio & Tannen, 1928

Young, Robert LI.D., Analytical Concordance of the Bible, New York, Funk & Wagnallls Company, 1936

Good News/New Testament published by American Bible Society 1977

Minister Asserts the Bible is Hoax, Guyana Chronicle, Sunday February 22,1987

Christmas, New York Daily News, Sunday December 23, 1979

Shroud of Turin Has Human DNA, New York Daily News, Sunday, March 29, 1998, Simon and Schuster, New York; 1962.

Order Form

For more information or wholesale requests, write:
Levitical Communications Inc.
P.O. Box 1324 - Bear, DE 19701

Check all that apply:

Title	Cost	Qty
❑ Israelites and Jews	$15.00	_______
❑ Final Resolution	$17.00	_______

Please send me the book(s) checked above at the total cost of $________.
Add $4.75 for shipping and handling (add $. 75 for each additional book).

Name: ____

Address: ____

City State, Zipcode: ________________________________

Please complete the form above, include the proper funds and mail to:
Levitical Communications Inc.
P.O. Box 1324 - Bear, DE 19701

For Credit Card Orders VISA, MASTERCARD, DISCOVER
or AMERICAN EXPRESS call (202) 291-0050.